A taste of
The Shires

A taste of
The Shires

First published 2003
by Midland Independent Magazines
Weaman Street, Birmingham B4 6AT

Editor: Fiona Alexander
Design Editor: Stacey Barnfield
Photography: Craig Holmes
Writer: Louise Palfreyman
Production Manager: Julia Gregory
Sales Manager: Zoe Austin
Sales Executive: Russel Hartland

All recipe suggestions © the restaurants
All images © Craig Holmes/Metro Photographic

British Library Cataloguing in Publication data:
a catalogue record for this book is available from The British Library

Also available: A Taste of Birmingham

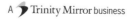

A Trinity Mirror business

A taste of
The Shires

Photography by Craig Holmes

CONTENTS

All dishes serve four unless stated otherwise

FOREWORD

This book has come together with the help and commitment of some of the finest establishments in the whole of England, and all of them from our own Midland counties.

England is internationally recognised as a centre of culinary excellence, and in my mind there is no place in the UK to compare with the central shires.

The area now draws huge numbers of tourists for a variety of reasons, but most definitely included is our gastro-prowess! The sleepy market town of Ludlow, in Shropshire where I am very lucky to now live, running the Overton Grange Hotel, has become the culinary capital of the UK with not only three Michelin-starred restaurants, and many more Michelin-listed, but also with a tremendous selection of pubs, restaurants and hotels who all care about food. They are passionate about their trade, and provide dishes created from the freshest and finest of mostly local ingredients in the most marvellous of surroundings, often with breath-taking views.

This care and passion extends not just through Shropshire, but throughout the other Midland counties. Whether you are looking for traditional fayre, or wanting to dip perhaps into the more exotic flavours and moods, there are establishments here that can provide you with the ultimate dining experience, and all within easy reach of Birmingham. We should all be very proud of our local reputation.

I hope that you will enjoy not just reading this book, but learning from it too... preparing and cooking the ingredients, sharing the finished product with close family and friends, and finally enjoy visiting the fine contributors to this book. So, read... eat... and enjoy!

Franck Choblet, Michelin-listed owner of Overton Grange Hotel

A taste of
The Shires

Dinner is served...

ALVESTON MANOR

ALVESTON MANOR

We're steeped in history here at Alveston where records of an actual hotel date back to before the Norman Conquest of 1066. Even before then, a monastery was recorded on the site.

There are many different periods of history in the house, from the Elizabethan panelling in the bar to the vaulted cellar under the lounge, and a hidden passage that was used by the monks all those centuries ago.

Even the gardens have their own story to tell – the cedar tree in the garden is reputed to be where Shakespeare held the first performance of A Midsummer Night's Dream. So there's plenty for diners to digest apart from our cuisine when they pay a visit.

I think I managed to bring a sense of attention to detail to our kitchens when I joined in 2000.

We have a large restaurant and I introduced a modern British style with the emphasis on traditional English dishes.

Being a manor house steeped in history, we feel that offering a combination of traditional grills, roasts and modern dishes achieves the right balance.

I source my ingredients from all over the country, and see an increase in the popularity of fish dishes, something I support having spent a year in Bournemouth cooking up local delights there.

A new chapter of history for us is the opening of our new leisure club which will see more people discovering the delights of our restaurant.

Richard Walton

Pressed roasted vegetable terrine, sundried tomato croute, aged balsamic reduction

INGREDIENTS

Sundried tomato bread – couple of slices per person

1 courgette

2 banana shallots

Half red, yellow and green pepper

12 cherry tomatoes

1 clove garlic

25ml olive oil

Mixed lettuce leaves

15ml balsamic vinegar

10g basil

Seasoning

METHOD

Line terrine mould with clingfilm or individual moulds and place in fridge.

Slice courgettes, peppers and fry in a little olive oil.

Bake courgettes and peppers in a hot oven.

Fry shallots and bake in oven.

Fry off cherry tomatoes with a little basil.

Layer different vegetables in your mould, topped with clingfilm and weigh it down. Leave overnight in fridge.

Slice or unwrap and present on a plate with mixed lettuce, toasted croutons (fried cubes of tomato bread), olive oil and balsamic vinegar.

Alveston Manor
Clopton Bridge, Stratford-upon-Avon, Warwickshire. CV37 6ER.
Tel: 01789 205478
gm.alvestonmanor@macdonald-hotels.co.uk   www.alvestonmanor.co.uk

ALVESTON MANOR

Flash fried loin of Scottish lamb, egg plant caviar, ratatouille of vegetables

INGREDIENTS

4 lamb loin 200g each

Ratatouille (mix of red pepper, yellow pepper, green pepper, aubergine, onion, courgette stewed in tomato juice)

Mashed potato – enough for 4 people

10g thyme

75ml red wine jus

25ml red currant jelly

1 aubergine

25ml olive oil

2 good-sized tomatoes

200ml tomato juice

2 cloves garlic

Salt and pepper to taste

METHOD

Make the ratatouille by cutting all the veg into similar shaped pieces and frying in a little oil then add tomato juice and bring to simmer.

Dry out thyme in a very low oven.

Cut aubergine, and bake with a little garlic and olive oil in a moderate oven until it is soft, scoop out and cook to dry out a bit. Add chopped parsley and diced tomato.

Seal lamb, season, and cook in oven until pink then take out and rest for a couple of minutes.

Heat mashed potato and mould into a round, do the same with the ratatouille Slice the lamb and present on either the mash or the ratatouille.

Napé the jus around the plate, garnish with the thyme on top.

Serve with the aubergine.

Alveston Manor
Clopton Bridge, Stratford-upon-Avon, Warwickshire. CV37 6ER.
Tel: 01789 205478
gm.alvestonmanor@macdonald-hotels.co.uk   www.alvestonmanor.co.uk

Chocolate and orange tort, pistachio tuille, vanilla pod ice cream

INGREDIENTS

Serves 5

140g chocolate (55% cocoa content)
275ml double cream

0.5ml golden syrup
14ml water
40ml orange juice
1.5 leaves bronze leaf gelatine

METHOD

Melt down chocolate, orange juice and golden syrup.

Whip cream to ribbon stage, leaving a little for dissolving the gelatine.

Put gelatine in water, and when chocolate is melted, take off the heat.

Mix the gelatine solution with a little bit of cream, and add to whipped cream.

Fold melted chocolate into whipped cream until thoroughly mixed.

Pipe into prelined moulds and allow to set.

Tuille basket: Equal quantities of melted butter, icing sugar, flour, egg whites (100g of each).

Mix together, spread out on a silicon mat to the shape you want and cook in a moderate oven for 4-6 minutes or until golden brown.

Serve tort with tuille basket and vanilla pod ice cream.

Alveston Manor
Clopton Bridge, Stratford-upon-Avon, Warwickshire. CV37 6ER.
Tel: 01789 205478
gm.alvestonmanor@macdonald-hotels.co.uk   www.alvestonmanor.co.uk

BRIDGE 59

BRIDGE 59

We've been at Bridge 59 for 18 months and consider that we've taken things up a notch.

A refurbishment and refit has brightened up the interior and we've gone for modern furnishings with a traditional edge.

Rainer, our chef, is Austrian so there is a little Austrian flavour in the food. He did his formal training in Austria followed by London at the Savoy and bought his first restaurant up in Saddleworth.

With our menu we've tried to keep in old favourites but with a modern twist. We do ostrich and frogs' legs, but also Beef Wellington.

Presentation is all important and we emphasise the seasonal, organic nature of our ingredients.

Our meat is sourced from local farms – we want customers to know where their dishes come from.

Our second chef Makesh Kumar started out with us and has trained up into an excellent chef. He's introduced Asian flavours in sauces and we now have a spicy edge to some dishes on the menu.

We find the fusion of East and West works well. It is, after all, very important to get that blend right when you are running a restaurant.

Jo Failoni

BRIDGE 59

Lamb salad scented with rosemary

INGREDIENTS

Serves 2 people

1 tenderloin of lamb 250g

2 sprigs Rosemary

3tbsp olive oil

1tbsp white wine vinegar

1 small aubergine

1 small courgette

1 tomato

1pkt of mixed salad leaves

METHOD

Marinate the lamb overnight with two sprigs of rosemary back and front and cover with two tablespoons of olive oil.

Sear lamb all over in the olive oil and roast in preheated oven 200°C for 5-7 minutes. Remove, then season with salt and pepper and set aside to rest.

Dice vegetables and pan-fry for 1-2 minutes.

Wash salad and place in centre of plate. Slice lamb and arrange around. Sprinkle the vegetables over. Make a vinaigrette with meat juices, one tablespoon of white wine vinegar and two tablespoons of olive oil. Drizzle over salad.

Bridge 59
5 Bridgnorth Road, Compton, Wolverhampton. WV6 8AB
Tel: 01902 759049
failonibridge59@hotmail.com

BRIDGE 59

Devonshire fish stew

INGREDIENTS

Serves 2 People

200g fresh mussels

1 fresh red sea bream filleted 150g

1 fresh sea bass filleted 150g

4 large prawns shell on

1 fresh dressed crab

500ml fish stock (available from supermarkets)

50g butter

100ml single cream

1 glass white wine

Small leek (just the white part)

Pinch of saffron

1 small glove garlic

1 tbsp tomato purée

Salt and pepper

METHOD

In a large saucepan sweat the shredded leek in the butter for 4-5 minutes. Add the crushed shell from the crab, the dark crab meat, tomato purée, and crushed garlic. Cook gently for a minute or two. Deglaze with a glass of white wine. Add fish stock and simmer gently for 20 minutes.

Season with salt and ground pepper and enrich with cream. Strain, add mussels, prawns, sea bass, red bream and saffron.

Simmer for 4-5 minutes and serve.

Bridge 59
5 Bridgnorth Road, Compton, Wolverhampton. WV6 8AB
Tel: 01902 759049
failonibridge59@hotmail.com

BRIDGE 59

Caramelised rice pudding with summer fruit compote

INGREDIENTS

Serves 2 people

30g short-grain rice

200ml milk

Vanilla pod (or essence)

40g sugar

1 whole egg

Rind of half lemon grated

Caramel

1 tbsp water

30g sugar

2 peaches or fruit in season

METHOD

Make the caramel. Combine sugar and water in a pan and cook until dark. Divide in two moulds.

Bring 150ml of milk to the boil. Add rice and vanilla pod simmer gently for 20 minutes until rice is soft. Leave to cool. Beat remaining milk, egg, lemon rind and sugar. Add to rice and stir. Place into moulds and bake in oven 200°C in a bain-marie for 20 minutes.

Bridge 59
5 Bridgnorth Road, Compton, Wolverhampton. WV6 8AB
Tel: 01902 759049
failonibridge59@hotmail.com

Epic' Bar Brasseries

Epic' Bar Brasseries

Michelin-starred chef Patrick McDonald and his wife Claire are the driving force behind Epic' Bar Brasseries.

The name Epic' was born out of Patrick's Michelin-starred restaurant "Epicurean".

Patrick's background naturally led him to focus on the style of food, setting the standard within Epic' Brasseries. Claire on the other hand continues to concentrate on the interior décor and Epic' brand.

The first Epic' Bar Brasserie opened in Bromsgrove at the beginning of April 2001, within the first six months it had been awarded a Michelin Bib Gourmand. Since then a further two restaurants have been added, the latest one in Dunhampton opened at the start of September this year. Additional Epic' Bar Brasseries are anticipated throughout the West Midlands in the next three years.

The aim at Epic' is simple; to create a relaxed accessible venue, that works for everyone from businessmen to families. There is a strong belief in the social and health benefits of using organic produce, a selection of organic wines and dishes are constantly available on the menu as an integral part of the brand.

Patrick says: "The essence of good food is simplicity and there is no substitute for the best quality ingredients presented well."

www.epicbrasseries.co.uk

Seared salmon Laksa

INGREDIENTS

4 x 100g pieces of salmon fillet

Laksa base

50g finely diced shallots

25g finely grated fresh root ginger

2 cloves garlic finely sliced

1 tin coconut milk

25ml Thai fish sauce

50ml sweet chilli sauce

2tsp Chinese five spice powder

125ml milk

4 lime leaves

2 sticks lemon grass

To garnish

200g cooked rice noodles

50g bean shoots

50g shiitake mushrooms finely sliced

50g shredded pak choi

1 bunch fresh coriander finely chopped

METHOD

Place all laksa base ingredients into a pan and bring to the boil. Once boiled remove from the heat and leave to infuse for 4 to 6 hours.

Once cool remove lime leaves and lemon grass.

In a hot non stick pan fry the salmon with a little olive oil and seasoning until a golden colour is achieved but the salmon is still pink in the centre.

To garnish: Reheat the laksa base and add the garnishing ingredients.

Place the cooked noodles in a serving bowl.

Add the laksa to the serving bowls and top with the seared piece of salmon.

Epic' Bar Brasserie (Bromsgrove)
68 Hanbury Road, Stoke Prior,
Bromsgrove, Worcestershire. B60 4DN
Tel: 01527 871929
epic.bromsgrove@virgin.net

Epic' Bar Brasserie (Whitacre Heath)
1 Station Road, Whitacre Heath,
Warwickshire. B46 2JA
Tel: 01675 462181
epic.whitacre@virgin.net

Epic' Bar Brasserie (Dunhampton)
The Half Way House, Dunhampton,
Worcestershire. DY13 9SW
Tel: 01905 620000
epic.dunhampton@virgin.net
www.epicbrasseries.co.uk

Epic' Bar Brasseries

Roast rump of lamb Provençale

INGREDIENTS

4 x 225-275g rumps of lamb

4 portion pomme fondant
4 large Estima potatoes
4oz butter
Salt and ground white pepper
Water

4 portions lamb sauce
1lb meat, diced
4 shallots, sliced

2 cloves of garlic, sliced
$1/_2$ pint veal stock
$1/_2$ pint double chicken stock
2tbsp olive oil

To garnish
100g large diced tomato
100g large diced aubergine
100g large diced courgette
100g halved black olives
I bunch diced fresh basil

METHOD

Season the lamb well. In a hot pan brown all over in olive oil then roast in a pre-heated oven 220°C for 8 to 10 minutes. Rest the meat for 10 to 15 minutes.

Lamb sauce: In a roasting tray, heat the oil and sear the meat, until golden brown turning frequently and place in a pre-heated oven to roast for one hour.

In a separate frying pan add the shallots and garlic, sauté over a moderate to high heat until light brown in colour. When the meat is roasted add the shallots and garlic.

Add the stocks and bring to the boil, skim and reduce the heat and simmer for 30-40 mins. Allow to rest for five minutes off the heat. Pass through a fine muslin cloth several times to remove any impurities for a wonderful clear sauce.

Pomme fondant: Peel the potatoes and flatten horizontally one side with a 2-3 inch round pastry cutter cut out a disc from each potato then with the remaining bevelled side cut this flat, the potatoes should all be the same depth and diameter.

In a heavy based saucepan layer the bottom of the pan with the butter, sit the potato discs on top, season with salt and pepper and add the cold water, just enough to level the top of the discs. Cook on a gentle heat until all the water has evaporated and the butter turns a nut brown and clarifies.

NB. Once on the stove don't move the potatoes or cover with a lid.

When ready remove from the heat and allow to rest for 20 minutes. This will give time to absorb the butter and aid release from the bottom of the pan.

To garnish: Bring the lamb sauce to the boil and add the garnishing ingredients.
Place a fondant potato on each serving plate.
Carve the lamb into six slices and arrange around the fondant potato.
Spoon over the sauce and serve.

Epic' Bar Brasserie (Bromsgrove)
68 Hanbury Road, Stoke Prior,
Bromsgrove, Worcestershire. B60 4DN
Tel: 01527 871929
epic.bromsgrove@virgin.net

Epic' Bar Brasserie (Whitacre Heath)
1 Station Road, Whitacre Heath,
Warwickshire. B46 2JA
Tel: 01675 462181
epic.whitacre@virgin.net

Epic' Bar Brasserie (Dunhampton)
The Half Way House, Dunhampton,
Worcestershire. DY13 9SW
Tel: 01905 620000
epic.dunhampton@virgin.net
www.epicbrasseries.co.uk

Epic' Bar Brasseries

Pineapple tart tatin with mango ice cream

INGREDIENTS

1 large pineapple skin removed

2 vanilla pods

4 star anise

200g unsalted butter

200g caster sugar

300g puff pastry

To garnish

4 portions mango ice cream

METHOD

Slice the pineapple into four equal slices and remove the core with a pastry cutter.

Caramelise the pineapple rings in the butter and caster sugar.

Place the pineapple rings and the caramel left over from caramelising into four small tartlet cases, add the vanilla pods and star anise and cover with the puff pastry discs.

Bake in a pre-heated (200ºC) oven for 15 minutes.

Turn the tarts out and serve with a ball of mango ice cream.

Epic' Bar Brasserie (Bromsgrove)
68 Hanbury Road, Stoke Prior,
Bromsgrove, Worcestershire. B60 4DN
Tel: 01527 871929
epic.bromsgrove@virgin.net

Epic' Bar Brasserie (Whitacre Heath)
1 Station Road, Whitacre Heath,
Warwickshire. B46 2JA
Tel: 01675 462181
epic.whitacre@virgin.net

Epic' Bar Brasserie (Dunhampton)
The Half Way House, Dunhampton,
Worcestershire. DY13 9SW
Tel: 01905 620000
epic.dunhampton@virgin.net
www.epicbrasseries.co.uk

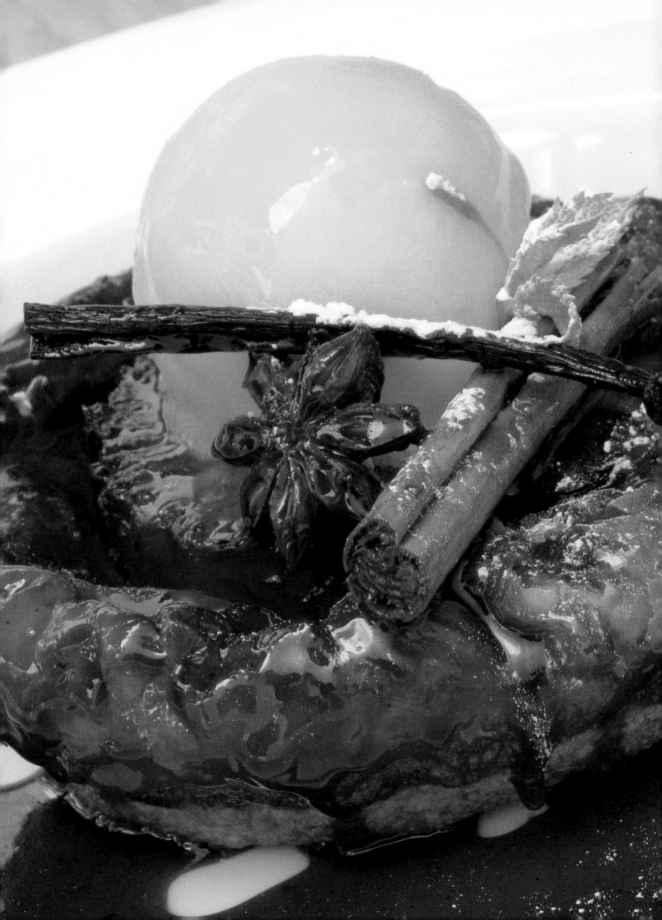

KAFFE FREDERIQUES

KAFFE FREDERIQUES

To try to find a restaurant which doesn't disappoint in one way or another is virtually unheard of today.

My vision for Frederiques, my first restaurant, was simply to create a restaurant which combines everything for the discerning customer.

Frederiques is a fine dining restaurant which I converted from a Spar shop. I employ three full time chefs. Tim Johns, my head chef has been with me since day one and has truly made the menu his own. Tim stipulates using only the best ingredients available and all dishes are cooked fresh to order. His imagination and flair for cooking is obvious in all his dishes. He is supported by two excellent chefs Mal Billingsley and Chris Wall.

Myself, Claire and Andrea (both of whom have again been with me since day one) support Tim's excellent food by giving our customers the excellent service they deserve. Our tables are candlelit with dimmed lighting and lively but unintrusive background music. My customers truly appreciate the no smoking policy and age restriction I have in place.

My aim is to please everyone, my customers are my business and I am pleased to say they continue to return and recommend Frederiques.

I am truly proud of all my long standing staff and that I am achieving all I set out to achieve.

I am sure if you enjoy excellent food in a lovely relaxed atmosphere, Frederiques is an experience you will want to sample again and again.

Jo Mills, Proprietor, Kaffe Frederiques Taverna

KAFFE FREDERIQUES

Chargrilled scallops, tomato, orange and rocket salad

INGREDIENTS

3 fresh king scallops

15g rocket leaves

50g plum tomatoes (peeled and deseeded)

35g orange (segmented)

10g red onion (finely diced)

10g cucumber

5g pitted black olives

5ml dressing (20ml olive oil, 15ml lemon juice, 5g grainy mustard, 1g black pepper)

METHOD

Cut the tomato into strips. Peel the cucumber and cut in half, scooping out the seeds, then slice. Mix with the rocket leaves, onion, olives and orange segments.

Lightly dress and stack up in the centre of the plate.

Chargrill the scallops quickly for 20 seconds on each side.

Place the scallops around the salad and drizzle with more dressing.

Season with sea salt.

Kaffe Frederiques
16 High Street, Albrighton, Wolverhampton. WV7 3JT
Tel: 01902 375522
jfrederiques@aol.co.uk

Poached monkfish in smoked salmon, seafood, greens and white wine cream

INGREDIENTS

150g monkfish	20g tomato concasse
2 slices smoked salmon	5g chopped dill
2 scallops	
2 mussels	**Court Bouillon**
2 king prawns	150ml water
2 clams	25ml lemon juice
100g savoy cabbage (finely shredded)	25ml white wine vinegar
20g butter	6 peppercorns
1 banana shallot	1 bay leaf
125ml double cream	1 sprig thyme

METHOD

Cook the cabbage in a pan of salted water then refresh.

Put all the court bouillon ingredients in a deep sided frying pan and bring to the boil.

Wrap the monkfish in the smoked salmon and place in the court bouillon. Simmer for 6-8 minutes, remove and keep warm.

Place all the seafood in the same pan and simmer for 2-3 minutes. Remove and keep warm.

Melt half the butter in a frying pan and fry the cabbage until hot. Place in the centre of a plate.

Peel and finely dice the shallot, sauté lightly, add the wine and two tablespoons of court bouillon, reduce down, add the double cream and simmer.

Add the other half of the butter and stir, take off the heat and add the herbs, stirring in.

Place the seafood round the cabbage, the monkfish on top. Spoon over the sauce and sprinkle with the tomato concasse.

Kaffe Frederiques
16 High Street, Albrighton, Wolverhampton. WV7 3JT
Tel: 01902 375522
jfrederiques@aol.co.uk

KAFFE FREDERIQUES

Chocolate and chilli crème brûlée

INGREDIENTS

25g demerara sugar

6 egg yolks

1 small chilli

300ml double cream

100g caster sugar

150g good quality chocolate

Raspberry coulis (shop-bought)

METHOD

Melt the chocolate over a bain-marie then keep warm.

In a small pan heat the cream with the deseeded chilli to boiling point. Take off the heat and in a suitable mixing bowl mix the egg yolk and sugar with a whisk. Slowly add the cream, stirring well at the same time.

Once the mixture resembles a thin custard whisk in the melted chocolate until smooth.

Pass through a fine sieve.

Pour into ramekins, leaving half and inch at the top.

Fill a deep baking tray with one inch of water and place the ramekins in the tray and bake for 20-25 minutes at 120ºC.

Remove from the oven and allow to cool. Refrigerate.

Sprinkle demerara sugar over the top of the custard mix and blow torch or grill until caramelised.

Serve with fresh fruits and a scoop of raspberry sauce.

Kaffe Frederiques
16 High Street, Albrighton, Wolverhampton. WV7 3JT
Tel: 01902 375522
jfrederiques@aol.co.uk

LEE GARDEN

LEE GARDEN

Lee Garden has been delighting diners for more than a decade.

I started out with a restaurant in Sutton Coldfield, which proved so popular that Lee Garden soon followed.

I brought over a chef from Hong Kong with a wealth of experience cooking both there and in Malaysia.

The restaurant specialises in Cantonese and Malaysian cuisine and has built up a loyal clientele over the years, with perhaps 70 per cent of business represented by returning customers. But Lichfield also plays host to many tourists, who often discover Lee Garden and are always pleasantly surprised.

People come to eat the traditional chicken and beef dishes, and many more enjoy seafood including monkfish, sea bass, scallops and king prawns. There is also a special menu for vegetarians.

The restaurant tries to avoid too many European dishes, but there are some basic chicken dishes available.

There is a function room for 60 people upstairs at Lee Garden, and the ground floor seats 80, making it an impressive size, with quality cuisine to match.

Tony Cheung

LEE GARDEN

Steamed seafood Shanghai dumplings

INGREDIENTS

150g uncooked peeled prawns

100g monkfish

30g bamboo shoots, finely chopped

1 tbsp finely chopped spring onions

30g crab roe

Salt and pepper

Won ton pastry (available in Chinese supermarkets)

A few strands of Kau Choi

Steamed dumplings are a very traditional oriental starter which are light enough to complement any main course. They are usually served with a touch of soy sauce for a mouthwatering experience.

METHOD

Mix the prawns, fish, bamboo shoots and onions in a large mixing bowl and season with salt and pepper.

Hold one slice of won ton pastry flat in the palm of the hand then place one tablespoon of seafood mixture into the middle of the pastry. Wrap the pastry around the filling, moistening the edges to stick.

Use one strand of Kau Choi to tie around the dumpling, then place a small amount of crab roe on the top edges.

Steam for six minutes, being careful not to overcook.

Lee Garden
50 Tamworth Street, Lichfield, Staffs. WS13 6JP
Tel: 01543 418515

LEE GARDEN

Stir fried lobster with ginger and spring onions

INGREDIENTS

800g fresh lobster (medium sized, shell on) cut into large pieces

1 bunch of spring onions, cut into $1^1/_2$" lengths

Half a small onion, thinly sliced

1 clove of garlic, finely chopped

2tbsp cornflour

Vegetable oil

Seasoning

1tbsp water

1tbsp oyster sauce

1tbsp cornflour

1tsp sugar

$^1/_2$tsp sesame oil

$^1/_4$tsp salt

METHOD

Mix the seasoning ingredients together in a small dish and place aside.

Sprinkle the cornflour over the lobster and deep fry in hot vegetable oil for one minute and drain, just to half cook the lobster, still in its shell.

Heat a tablespoon of oil in a wok, add the garlic and ginger for a couple of seconds, then add the lobster. Stir for a minute, add a cup of water and cover with a lid for six minutes. Stir the seasoning.

Remove the lid, stir in the spring onions and seasoning, then cook for another two minutes, stirring.

Serve immediately.

Lee Garden
50 Tamworth Street, Lichfield, Staffs. WS13 6JP
Tel: 01543 418515

LEE GARDEN

Toffee banana with ice cream

INGREDIENTS

Batter Mix

10tbsp flour

1 egg

Water

2 bananas cut into four pieces

Sugar

Sesame seeds

50ml ice cream

METHOD

Mix the flour and egg, add water to make a thick batter.

Dip the banana pieces in the batter then deep fry until golden brown and drain.

Heat a teaspoon of oil in a wok, add two tablespoons of sugar, stirring until melted. Add four pieces of the fried banana.

Coat with the toffee mixture then place on a baking tray, sprinkling with sesame seeds. Repeat for the rest of the banana.

Leave to stand for two minutes and serve with ice cream.

Lee Garden
50 Tamworth Street, Lichfield, Staffs. WS13 6JP
Tel: 01543 418515

NAILCOTE HALL

NAILCOTE HALL

Nailcote Hall is a 17th century gem tucked away in rolling countryside. Chosen by the AA as one of Great Britain and Ireland's most romantic hotels it features The Oak Room, one of the most delightful and intimate restaurants in the Heart of England.

For lunch or dinner, the table d'hôte menus of the day offer a well balanced selection of the best of modern international cuisine and there is always a vegetarian choice as well as a simple selection of grills.

New head chef Neil Oates, above, is hoping to bring his own style and interpretation to the already AA two-rosetted Oak Room Restaurant.

The Oak Room is a traditional setting and so we don't go in too much for modern fusion cuisine. Our customers appreciate the subtleties of grilled Dover sole or steak or salmon nicely cooked.

We use only the finest fresh ingredients and, where possible source them locally.

At Nailcote we are able to offer them a varied and extensive, well thought out menu.

Rick Cressman, Nailcote Hall

NAILCOTE HALL

Fillet of brill with a crab and Berkswell cheese rarebit, carpaccio of vine tomatoes

INGREDIENTS

4 x 90g brill supremes

4 ripe vine tomatoes

Sea salt

Black pepper

Good olive oil

2 slices brioche

Rarebit

60g white crab meat

1 egg yolk

2tbsp thick béchamel sauce

1tsp chopped herbs (tarragon, chervil, parsley, dill)

120ml stout or ale reduced to one tsp

$^1/_2$tsp English mustard

80g Berkswell cheese, grated

METHOD

Slice the tomatoes as thinly as possible (for best results use an electric slicer), lay on a tray and season with sea salt, pepper and olive oil. Leave to marinate.

Heat the béchamel, stirring until smooth, add the cheese and mustard, then the ale reduction. Remove from the heat and cool slightly before adding the egg yolk and then finally the crab meat and herbs.

Season the brill and place in a buttered ovenproof dish.

Spoon the rarebit mix generously on top of the brill and cook in a hot oven for four to five minutes.

Toast the brioche and cut into four squares.

To serve: Arrange the sliced tomatoes, overlapping in a circular fashion on serving plates.

At the centre of each plate, place a square of brioche and on top of this carefully place the brill rarebit (which should be browned).

Drizzle the plates with a little olive oil and serve.

Notes: Berkswell cheese is a hard cheese made from unpasteurised sheep's milk made at Ram Hall farm on the outskirts of Berkswell. It is available locally or via the internet. Pecorino cheese or Gruyére are both good substitutes.

Nailcote Hall Hotel
Nailcote Lane, Berkswell, Warwickshire. CV7 7DE
Tel: 024 7646 6174
info@nailcotehall.co.uk   www.nailcotehall.co.uk

Herb crusted Cornish lamb, confit of shoulder, sweetbread pithivier, glazed baby turnips

INGREDIENTS

1 x 6 bone rack of lamb

2tbsp fresh breadcrumbs

2tsp chopped herbs (parsley, tarragon, rosemary and thyme)

1tsp Dijon mustard mixed with a little egg yolk

4 discs confit shoulder

4tsp shallot compote

4tsp cooked haricot beans bound with a little cream

4 halved cherry tomatoes

4 cooked halved baby artichokes

4 cloves garlic confit

12 pieces baby turnip

Pithivier

60g lamb's sweetbreads blanched, sautéed and glazed with Madeira

40g young spinach, picked, washed, wilted and pressed dry

150g puff pastry

300g creamed potatoes

200ml lamb jus

METHOD

To make the confit rub the shoulder of lamb with sea salt and rosemary. Leave in the fridge for 24 hours. Wash, cover with duck fat, cook for four hours at 95ºC. Remove, cool and pick meat from the bones, mix flaked meat with a little lamb jus and season.

Roll into sausage shape in clingfilm and chill.

Next make the shallot compote. Slice the shallots and cook gently in duck fat until tender, drain, return to the pan and increase heat to lightly brown.

Cut the tomatoes in half and lay on a baking tray, sprinkle with sea salt, chopped rosemary and powdered orange zest and leave to dry in a warm place.

Prepare and cook the baby artichokes in vegetable stock with white wine and coriander seeds.

Blanch the garlic cloves three times in water then cover in duck fat and cook slowly.

Prepare the baby turnips, cover with cold water, add a knob of butter, a pinch of salt and two pinches of sugar and simmer until cooked and the liquor reduces to a glaze.

For the pithivier, roll out the pastry to 2mm thick, cut four discs 6cm wide and four discs 8cm wide, divide the spinach and place on the smaller discs, repeat the process with the sweetbreads, brush the edges of the pastry with egg wash, place the larger discs on top and seal the edges.

Score the raised pastry with a knife and bake for 12 minutes at 160ºC.

Roast the rack of lamb in a hot oven until just pink, rest for 15 minutes then brush the fat side with the mustard mix.

Warm the confit shoulder in the oven.

Combine the herbs and breadcrumbs in a food processor for two minutes. Coat the fat side of the lamb with the herb crust and place under the grill to lightly toast.

To serve: Pipe the creamed potato at the centre of four serving plates.

Place a pithivier on each plate, then a spoonful of warmed haricot beans. On top of this place a warmed disc of confit shoulder, topped by a teaspoon of shallot compote.

Carve the rack into four even cutlets, discarding the outer bones. Arrange the cutlets on a pile of warmed artichoke, cherry tomato confit and garlic confit.

Dress with the lamb jus and serve.

Nailcote Hall Hotel
Nailcote Lane, Berkswell, Warwickshire. CV7 7DE
Tel: 024 7646 6174
info@nailcotehall.co.uk   www.nailcotehall.co.uk

NAILCOTE HALL

A trio of quintessentially English desserts

INGREDIENTS

Queen of puddings
250ml milk
Zest and juice of one lemon
60g butter
60g sugar
6 egg yolks
120g cake crumbs
120g Italian meringue
60g strawberry jam
4 raspberries

Stewed apple
Five Cox's apples
950ml water
225g sugar
Juice of half a lemon
6 cloves
1tsp vanilla essence
1 cinnamon stick

Summer pudding
120g strawberries
30g raspberries
30g blackberries
30g redcurrants
30g blueberries
18 slices white bread
60g sugar
250ml berry coulis

Crumble
120g sugar
120g butter
240g flour
60g ground almonds

To garnish
Apple tea ice cream
Clotted cream, sweetened with sugar and vanilla seeds, sprigs of mint

METHOD

Queen of puddings: Boil the milk and butter. Cream the sugar, yolks, zest and lemon juice, add to the milk and thicken slightly.

Add the cake crumbs and pour into small moulds. Cook for 10-15 minutes at 100°C in a bain marie. Cool, then top with a spot of jam, then pipe a swirl of meringue. Bake in a moderate oven until golden.

Summer pudding: Cut the large berries in half and sprinkle with sugar.

Boil the coulis and pour over the berries, leave to cool.

Flatten the bread slightly, cut into fingers and soak in the coulis.

Line small darioles (moulds) with clingfilm then line with the bread, overlapping the fingers. Fill with the berry mix, fold over the remaining bread to seal the mixture in.

Cover the moulds with a tray and press firmly overnight in the fridge.

Stewed apple crumble: Slice the tops off four of the apples, scoop out the flesh discarding only the core.

Peel and core the remaining apple and stew down with the scooped apple and a little of the sugar to sweeten.

Boil the water with the remaining ingredients, add the four hollowed apples, gently poach for five minutes until just tender but retaining their shape.

Rub together all the ingredients for the crumble until it resembles golden breadcrumbs.

Fill the hollowed apples with the stewed apple and top with a generous sprinkling of crumble then bake in a moderate oven until golden.

To serve: Turn out the summer puddings, glaze with any leftover coulis, and place a teaspoon of the vanilla clotted cream on top, along with a sprig of mint. Place these on a serving plate.

Place the Queen of Puddings and Apple Crumble either side of the Summer Pudding, place a small scoop of apple tea ice cream on top of the crumble and serve.

Nailcote Hall Hotel
Nailcote Lane, Berkswell, Warwickshire. CV7 7DE
Tel: 024 7646 6174
info@nailcotehall.co.uk   www.nailcotehall.co.uk

OVERTON GRANGE

OVERTON GRANGE

When you are concerned with offering the best, you have to employ the best. And so Louise and Franck Choblet were delighted to welcome Olivier Bossut to Overton Grange as head chef last November.

Ludlow has become nationally and internationally renowned as a gastronomic hotspot.

Food critics continue to wax lyrical about standards that put many London establishments to shame. And the presence of Overton Grange has certainly aided the reputation of this historic town in the highest food circles.

As the couple themselves state: "We believe fine food should taste as good as it looks and in our award winning AA 3 Rosette, Michelin Listed Restaurant we want your meal to be a sensory experience, a supreme combination of aromas, colours and most importantly, tastes."

The restaurant at Overton Grange consistently sets the standards for the area.

Olivier Bossut is dedicated to producing fine innovative cuisine. Every item on the carefully composed menu is chosen for its seasonal freshness and complimentary flavours.

The Grange itself is steeped in history. There has been a building on the site since 1066, as recorded in the Domesday Book. The present house was built in 1905 for the Betton-Foster Family.

Franck Choblet concludes: "Dining in the Edwardian panelled dining room with the high standard of service and cuisine is, we believe, an experience to savour."

www.overtongrangehotel.com

Bourguignon of scallops, baby leaf and white truffle salad

INGREDIENTS

12 to 20 scallops (depending on size)

Sea salt & black pepper

Olive oil

Sauce

2 shallots, finely chopped

20ml port

20ml Madeira wine

20ml cognac

20ml strong red wine

Beef stock (or half beef stock cube)

Unsalted butter

Pinch of chopped parsley

500g baby leaf salad

White truffle shavings

Regiano parmesan shavings

4tbsp white truffle oil

2tbsp aged balsamic vinegar

METHOD

Clean the salad leaves. Make a dressing by mixing the truffle oil and balsamic vinegar. Add salt and freshly ground pepper.

Season the scallops with salt and pepper and shallow pan-fry in hot oil for about one and half minutes on each side. Remove scallops and keep warm, pour the fat out of the pan and add the shallots, port, Madeira, cognac, wine and beef stock. Reduce liquid to thick sauce, and then pass through a fine sieve. Add the chopped parsley.

To serve: arrange scallops around the plate. Toss the salad leaves in the salad dressing and put in centre of plate. Sprinkle with parmesan and white truffle shavings. Drizzle the sauce over the scallops.

Overton Grange Hotel
Old Hereford Road, Ludlow, Shropshire. SY8 4AD
Tel: 01584 873500
info@overtongrangehotel.com

OVERTON GRANGE

Ballotine of quail with langoustine and ginger nut

INGREDIENTS

4 quail

1 poached William pear

100g of fresh foie gras

100g of caul fat

Sea salt and black pepper

8 walnut kernels

12 small ginger nuts (or piece of fresh ginger)

190g caster sugar

170ml water

22g glucose

12 langoustines

12 baby leeks

Unsalted butter

Olive oil

Sea salt and black pepper

100ml port

One cube chicken stock

METHOD

Bone the quail and remove the legs (or ask your butcher to prepare them for you).

Carefully make an opening along the back and open up gently. Inside each bird put quarter of pear, 25g foie gras, 2 walnut kernels and season with salt and freshly ground pepper. Wrap the caul fat around the bird to keep the shape.

To make the confit: Put the ginger nuts in a small saucepan (if using fresh ginger, peel and cut into small pieces). Boil with sugar, water and glucose to 110°C to make thick syrup. Leave to cool.

Remove the shells from the langoustines and clean by gently pulling out the black thread running through the tails.

Clean the leeks.

In a shallow frying pan melt the butter and oil and gently cook the quails breast side down for a few minutes until browned. Put into low oven (150°C) for 10-12 minutes to cook. Pour the fat away from the pan and add the port, chicken stock cube and two tablespoons of the ginger confit. Boil gently until reduced to a thick sauce. In another frying pan add olive oil, butter, salt and pepper and gently pan-fry the langoustines.

Steam baby leeks until 'al dente', and then glaze with olive oil.

To finish: On each plate make a circle in the centre with baby leeks. Carefully open each quail to show the pear and foie gras inside and put onto leeks. Add langoustines and ginger nuts around the plate and spoon on sauce.

Overton Grange Hotel
Old Hereford Road, Ludlow, Shropshire. SY8 4AD
Tel: 01584 873500
info@overtongrangehotel.com

White chocolate croustillant, confit of kumquats

INGREDIENTS

White chocolate mousse

1 vanilla pod

125ml of milk

125ml of whipping cream

2 egg yolks

2.5g of gelatine leaf

240g white chocolate

325ml of whipped cream

Croustilliant

37g unsalted butter

50g icing sugar

15g plain flour

Juice of one orange

Zest of one orange

32g glucose

10g golden syrup

Pinch of ground ginger

Confit

250g of kumquats, halved

1 passion fruit

170g caster sugar

150ml water

22g glucose

METHOD

White chocolate mousse: Boil milk and cream in saucepan with vanilla pod. Add chocolate, egg yolks and gelatine. Mix well then leave to cool. Fold in whipped cream. Put into fridge for about two hours to set.

Confit: Make using water, sugar and glucose and bring to the boil until 106°C. Spoon out centre of passion fruit and add to syrup. Add kumquats. Bring to the boil and take off heat. Leave to cool.

Croustilliant: Cream butter and icing sugar. In saucepan heat orange juice and zest, golden syrup and glucose. Pour onto butter, add flour and ground ginger and beat to make paste. Cool. Roll into very small balls and put onto tray in cool oven (150°C). Cook for about two and half minutes until golden brown.

The balls will melt into flat circles.

To serve: Layer croustillant with quenelles of chocolate mousse to make tower. Spoon confit syrup onto plate.

Overton Grange Hotel
Old Hereford Road, Ludlow, Shropshire. SY8 4AD
Tel: 01584 873500
info@overtongrangehotel.com

PIZZA ORGANIC

PIZZA ORGANIC

Pizza Organic was created in 1999 in answer to the emerging demand for organic food and the lack of organic restaurants.

Pizza Organic is certified by the Soil Association and is now the largest group of organic restaurants in the UK. Our aim is to provide freshly prepared food that is tasty, healthy and affordable, in stylish surroundings.

The menu offers a range of stonebaked pizzas, pastas and grills. All our food is organic (with the odd exception if not available) and is GM-free.

We try to source from local independent suppliers and constantly develop new recipes to make best use of seasonal varieties.

Pizza Organic Warwick is a stunning blend of modern design set inside a 16th century listed building. There are several atmospheric rooms suitable for an intimate meal for two, or for exclusive parties.

Details of our other restaurants can be found at our website www.pizzaorganic.co.uk

We look forward to welcoming you...

Jane Sharp, Pizza Organic

PIZZA ORGANIC

Organic cherry tomato bruschetta

INGREDIENTS

Serves 4-6

1 organic loaf or ciabatta

1 pack organic cherry tomatoes

4dsp organic olive oil

2oz organic pesto

$^1/_2$tsp sea salt

$^1/_2$tsp ground organic black pepper

Fresh organic basil leaves

METHOD

Cut the cherry tomatoes in half and place in a bowl.

Add the olive oil, salt, pepper and some torn basil leaves (the mixture can be left in the fridge for up to 24 hours to allow flavour to develop, but bring to room temperature before using).

When ready, cut the loaf into thick slices and toast both sides. Cut each slice diagonally in half and spread with a little pesto.

Place bread on serving plate and portion tomato mix on top. Garnish with fresh basil and serve.

Pizza Organic
33 Jury Street, Warwick. CV34 4EH
Tel: 01926 491641
info@pizzapiazza.co.uk   www.pizza-organic.co.uk

PIZZA ORGANIC

Organic pizza Margherita

Makes 4 pizzas

Dough

400g organic strong white flour

2tsp sea salt

1tsp organic sugar

2tbsp organic sunflower oil

1 packet easy blend dried yeast

225ml hot water approx

Pizza sauce

1 x 400g tin organic chopped tomatoes

50g organic tomato purée

Pinch sea salt

Pinch organic (dried oregano)

Topping

250g organic mozzarella or 2 organic mozzarella balls

Fresh organic basil

Organic black pepper

Mix the flour, salt and yeast. Make a well in the centre, pour in the oil and enough water to mix to a soft, slightly sticky dough.

Flour your hands and the work surface and knead the dough for 8-10 minutes until smooth and elastic.

Place in a clean bowl, cover with a damp cloth and leave in a warm place to prove for about an hour – it should double in size.

Meanwhile prepare the sauce and any toppings.

Drain any excess fluid from the tomatoes. Add purée, salt and oregano and mix together.

Dice the mozzarella into half inch cubes.

Store sauce and cheese in the fridge until required.

When the dough has doubled in size knock down with your fist and knead for a few minutes. Divide the dough into four and roll out each piece into a thin circle about 10 inch diameter. Place each on a lightly oiled baking sheet or non-stick tray.

Spread with pizza sauce, leaving a 1 inch rim.

Scatter the mozzarella over and sprinkle with oregano. Other toppings can be added but do not overtop the pizza or it will not cook properly.

Bake on the top shelf in a preheated oven gas mark 7/220°C for about 12 minutes until the crust is golden. If cooking two pizzas, move from one shelf to another at about seven minutes to ensure even cooking.

Scatter with fresh basil leaves, grind some black pepper over and serve on a large plate.

The pizza can be frozen once made up and kept for a month before cooking. Defrost at room temperature and cook as above.

Pizza Organic
33 Jury Street, Warwick. CV34 4EH
Tel: 01926 491641
info@pizzapiazza.co.uk   www.pizza-organic.co.uk

PIZZA ORGANIC

Organic banoffee pie

INGREDIENTS

Serves 8

250g organic digestive biscuits
125g organic butter
1 jar confiture or banoffee toffee or
dulche de leche (not available
organically)

3 organic bananas
1 small pot organic double cream
Sprinkle organic chocolate powder

METHOD

Crush the biscuits to a fine crumb. Melt the butter and mix together with the
crumbs. Pack evenly in a 10 inch flan tin and refrigerate until firm.

Remove from tin and place on a serving plate.

Spread the confiture evenly over the base.

Slice the bananas and place on top.

Lightly whip the cream and cover the top. Sprinkle with chocolate powder and
place a slice of banana on each portion.

Pizza Organic
33 Jury Street, Warwick. CV34 4EH
Tel: 01926 491641
info@pizzapiazza.co.uk   www.pizza-organic.co.uk

QUARTO'S

QUARTO'S

There's been a restaurant within the Royal Shakespeare Theatre for decades, as some of the most loyal clientele will testify. People have been coming here to eat since the 1950s and we've had politicians, Prince Charles, and of course many a famous actor through the doors.

In recent times we've sought to modernise and bring ourselves in line with the very best restaurants the region has to offer. Quarto's has been with the RSC for three years now. I was brought in to raise standards, and think it's safe to say we've achieved that.

Our menu reflects the global clientele we receive every day at the restaurant. So many nationalities visit Stratford and the RSC, and we offer classical dishes with a twist, with the emphasis on flavour.

We also cater for younger diners who may be visiting to see one of the children's productions, and produce themed menus filled with references to the show in question. The interior has undergone an extensive redesign, and we've probably got the best views in Stratford-Upon-Avon.

Quarto's overlooks the swans on the river and you can watch the world go by from the window as you eat.

We are always busy when a celebrated actor or actress is appearing in a production. But increasingly we're welcoming people at lunchtimes and outside traditional 'pre' or 'post' theatre times.

The Royal Shakespeare Theatre is the most famous in the world, and there's been a theatre on this site since 1879. The present theatre opened in 1932, and has gradually been extended to include the Swan and the Other Place.

But people don't just expect to see a play when they come here, and we offer them an added experience.

Carl Swift, Head Chef

QUARTO'S

Layered vegetable terrine

INGREDIENTS

For 10 servings

5 red peppers

5 yellow peppers

5 green peppers

5 courgettes

1 aubergine

2 punnets baby sweetcorn

5 carrots

5 leaves gelatine

600ml vegetable stock

METHOD

Slice courgette, aubergine and baby sweetcorn lengthways, season with olive oil, salt and roast in the oven.

Cut and de-seed peppers, season and roast these in the oven. Whilst vegetables are roasting, prepare your vegetable stock and leave to cool.

Soak gelatine in a little cold water and add to vegetable stock as it cools.

Remove vegetables from oven and leave to cool. Peel skin off peppers.

Layer vegetables in alternative colours in a lined terrine mould. Cover with vegetable stock and gelatine mixture to top of mould. Press with a heavy weight and refrigerate for 24 hours.

To serve: Slice generously and top with baby salad leaves.

Serve with drizzled balsamic vinegar and fresh herb oil.

Serve as required.

Quarto's
Royal Shakespeare Theatre, Waterside, Stratford-upon-Avon,
Warwickshire. CV37 6BB
Tel: 01789 403415
quartos@eliance.org.uk   www.rsc.org.uk/booking/stratford/restaurantsbars/

QUARTO'S

Assiette of seafood

INGREDIENTS

For 4 servings

4 x 5cm squares of salmon

4 x 5cm squares of red mullet

4 x 5cm squares of sea bass

4 x fresh king scallops

Sauce

120ml fish stock

3 shallots (finely diced)

60ml double cream

Dash of white wine

Good pinch of saffron

Juice of half lemon

15g unsalted butter

Garnish

20 cooked mussels

400g fresh spinach

White of 1 leek (cut into strips and deep fried)

METHOD

Place shallots, fish stock and dash of white wine into pan and reduce until syrupy, add saffron and cream and bring to boil.

Remove sauce from heat and blend in the butter, season with pepper and lemon juice and keep warm.

Roast fish in a little olive oil until just firm to touch (do not overcook).

To serve: Place a mound of cooked spinach on a plate, surround with fish and mussels in a half shell, add a little sauce and top with deep fried leek.

Serve with steamed new potatoes and fine French beans.

Quarto's
Royal Shakespeare Theatre, Waterside, Stratford upon Avon, Warwickshire. CV37 6BB
Tel: 01789 403415
quartos@eliance.org.uk   www.rsc.org.uk/booking/stratford/restaurantsbars/

Chocolate ricotta tart

INGREDIENTS

350g ricotta cheese

85g caster sugar

3 eggs

60g chopped mixed peel

60g nibbled almonds

Grated zest and juice of 1 lemon and
$1/2$ orange

4 drops vanilla essence

100g dark chocolate drops

Sweet pastry

400g soft flour

340g butter

6 egg yolks

285g icing sugar

To garnish

1 strawberry halved/fanned

1 sprig of mint

Kernel of coconut sorbet

METHOD

First make the pastry. Cream the butter and flour together, then add the icing sugar and mix in, add the egg and blend in until you get a smooth paste. Then refrigerate until needed.

Ensure there is no excess water on the ricotta, strain if necessary.

Place the ricotta into a mixing bowl and slowly mix in the sugar and the eggs with a spoon, gradually add the zest and juice. Add the almonds and mixed peel, stirring continuously. Add the vanilla essence and the chocolate drops.

Once all the ingredients are well mixed chill in the fridge.

Remove the prepared pastry from the fridge and roll on a floured cool surface to about 5ml. Place pastry into a 10 inch (tart pan/ring with loose bottom). Cut away any excess pastry. Pour the ricotta mixture into pastry case and smooth evenly.

Bake in the oven for 45-50 minutes at 180°C/350°C gas mark 4.
Garnish.

Quarto's
Royal Shakespeare Theatre, Waterside, Stratford upon Avon,
Warwickshire. CV37 6BB
Tel: 01789 403415
quartos@eliance.org.uk   www.rsc.org.uk/booking/stratford/restaurantsbars/

SAFE BAR & RESTAURANT

SAFE BAR & RESTAURANT

Safe has injected a modern flavour into the heart of historic Bridgnorth.

We were taken with the Georgian façade of the site we chose on the corner of the town's magnificent East Castle Street. But we wanted to ensure diners would enjoy the best of both traditional and contemporary styling, and the interior oozes comfort.

Safe, we feel it's safe to say, is set to become one of the region's gastronomic gems.

We've tried to create an oasis of contemporary chic within a Georgian, gentrified setting.

Sumptuous leather seating, oak flooring, and ivory voile drapes create the perfect balance of style and comfort.

The bar is a venue in its own right and we feel confident it will become a favourite rendezvous.

Move upstairs and the cuisine prepared by our chef Som Miller in the restaurant is quite simply divine. His inspired menu includes goat's cheese wonton with avocado salsa and sweet roast pepper sauce; and seared fillet of salmon, scallops and prawn beignets, potato galette and crayfish sauce.

For a corporate lunch, intimate dinner or birthday celebration, Safe is as close to perfection as it gets.

Safe Bar & Restaurant is open every day from 9am to midnight; Sunday lunch is served all day – children are welcome.

Owners Caroline Davis and Adam Raybould

Goat's cheese wontons

INGREDIENTS

100g firm goat's cheese, crumbled

6 x yellow Chinese wonton pastry sheets

Finely chopped coriander leaves

1 egg yolk

2 cups vegetable oil for frying

100g avocado, diced

80g red onion, diced

80g tomato, diced

2tbsp olive oil

Juice of half a lemon

Finely chopped coriander leaves

2tbsp Thai sweet chilli sauce

2tbsp olive oil

2tbsp lemon juice

2tbsp dark rich soy sauce (optional)

1oz mixed lettuce leaves

METHOD

Place the crumbled goat's cheese in the centre of each wonton pastry, then add a pinch of chopped coriander. Use egg yolk to seal the ends of each pastry, and then fold into a triangle and seal tight.

Heat vegetable oil until medium hot, then place wontons parcels in and fry until crispy (about 30 seconds each side). Take wontons out and drain, set aside until needed.

Mix the avocado, red onions, tomatoes together with olive oil, lemon juice and chopped coriander. Add a pinch of salt and pepper to taste and set aside until needed

Mix Thai sweet chilli sauce, olive oil and lemon juice, and then set aside until needed.

Place the avocado mixture in the centre of a plate, then top with wonton parcels and drizzle Thai sweet chilli sauce mixture around the plate with dark rich soy sauce (optional). Finish with mixed leaf lettuce dressed with a little olive oil on top of wontons.

Safe Bar & Restaurant
33 East Castle Street, Bridgnorth, Shropshire. WV16 4AM
Tel: 01746 765999

SAFE BAR & RESTAURANT

Roasted breast of duck with shiitake mushroom risotto, purple broccoli and spiced mango sauce

INGREDIENTS

1 large duck breast, clean then dry

2tbsp olive oil

Fresh black peppercorn, ground

Coarse sea salt

1tsp caster sugar

2tbsp Kikkoman soy sauce

$^1/_2$ cup risotto rice

1 cup shiitake mushrooms, roughly chopped

2 shallots, finely chopped

1 clove garlic, finely chopped

1 cup white wine

4 cups boiling hot chicken stock

Salt and pepper

Parmesan cheese (optional)

1 bok choi, trimmed and steamed

Purple broccoli stem, trimmed and steamed

1tsp Thai red curry paste

1 cup mango purée

$^1/_2$ cup orange juice

Salt

Spring onions, chopped

Coriander leaves

METHOD

Marinate the duck breast with above ingredients, and stand covered in the fridge for 1 hour. Preheat oven at 180°C and then heat oil in frying pan until slightly smoking. Place duck breast skin-side down and sear for 1 minute then turn and sear for another minute the other side. Transfer the duck breast to a small roasting pan skin side down and bake for 15 minutes for medium done and 20 for well done. Let the breast rest for 6-10 minutes.

Place the saucepan on medium heat and add olive oil, shallots and garlic. Cook until soft, then add mushrooms. Cook for two minutes then add rice heat for another two minutes. Add the white wine and one cup of the chicken stock. Continue to cook the rice adding one cup of chicken stock at a time until the risotto becomes tender. Let cool to set until needed.

In a small saucepan heat a little oil with red curry sauce for one minute, then add mango purée and orange juice and simmer for five minutes. Season with salt and pepper to taste.

Place risotto in a ring mould on the centre of a large dinner plate, place the steamed vegetables on top. Cut the duck breast into medium slices and lay across the risotto and vegetables. Heat sauce and spoon over and around the duck breast, garnish with spring onions and fresh coriander leaves.

Safe Bar & Restaurant
33 East Castle Street, Bridgnorth, Shropshire. WV16 4AM
Tel: 01746 765999

SAFE BAR & RESTAURANT

Mixed berries Napoleon

INGREDIENTS

3 yellow Chinese party sheets

1tsp caster sugar

1 cup of vegetable oil for frying

2tbsp caster sugar

3tbsp water, hot

Lime juice

3 star anise

150g raspberries

150g blueberries

200g strawberries

250g cream cheese, softened

100g sour cream

150g icing sugar

2tbsp rum

Raspberry coulis

White chocolate sauce

Fresh mint leaves

METHOD

Heat the vegetable oil in saucepan over medium heat, fry wonton pastry (party sheets) until crispy (about one minute). Take pastry out and dust with caster sugar on both side until coated. Set aside until needed.

Mix hot water, caster sugar, lime juice and star anise until liquid becomes clear, let stand until liquid becomes cool and then blend in the berries. Set aside until needed.

Blend cream cheese, sour cream, icing sugar and rum until smooth.

On the centre of plate place a spoonful of cream cheese mixture, then one wonton pastry, then a spoonful of berries. Continue this two more times with wonton to finish on top. Garnish with raspberry coulis and white chocolate and mint leaves.

Safe Bar & Restaurant
33 East Castle Street, Bridgnorth, Shropshire. WV16 4AM
Tel: 01746 765999

SWINFEN HALL HOTEL

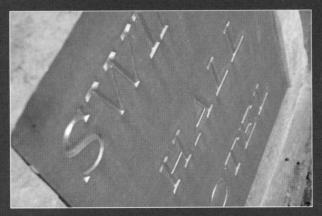

SWINFEN HALL HOTEL

When we bought Swinfen Hall it was a semi-derelict manor house lying in six acres of overgrown gardens. Fifteen years on it is a very beautiful hotel amid 100 acres of rolling Staffordshire parkland.

Our vision for the restaurant was simple – good quality imaginative food, beautiful surroundings and a friendly and relaxed atmosphere. The food may be the pearl in the oyster but eating out should be a total experience.

We have a dedicated kitchen brigade led by Neil Peers. Neil first joined the hotel in 1998 and became Head Chef in 2000. His style of cooking is modern European but he incorporates ideas and influences from around the world. Neil's dishes are based on classic concepts but developed with imagination and style.

Good quality ingredients are the basis of good food and the kitchen brigade work hard to source independent producers committed to their cause. Wherever possible we use local suppliers and we are now developing our own kitchen gardens.

In the summer, you can sit on the terrace and enjoy beautiful views running down to the lake. In the winter, you can toast by a roaring log fire, but whatever the season we promise you fine food in surroundings of unashamed luxury.

Helen and Vic Wiser, Swinfen Hall Hotel

Hot smoked salmon with crab and avocado

INGREDIENTS

500g fresh salmon fillet

120g flaked white crab meat

1 tbsp crème fraiche

1 avocado

150ml double cream

1 tsp lemon juice

12 well trimmed asparagus spears
(use wild when in season)

Olive oil

Seasoning

1 tsp salmon caviar (optional)

Herb pancake mixture

Make a standard pancake batter but
add a handful of chopped mixed herbs

METHOD

Whip the double cream until it starts to stiffen. Peel and stone the avocado and mix in a food processor until smooth. Add the lemon juice and seasoning. Fold in the cream and chill.

Cut the fresh salmon into circles using a one and three quarter inch ring cutter and rub all over with oil and then season. Place a wok on the stove over a medium heat and put in one handful of smoking wood chips. Place a metal gauze in the wok and put the salmon circles on this. Cover with foil and cook for 5-6 minutes until lightly browned.

Mix the flaked crab with seasoning and crème fraiche and press into a one and quarter inch ring cutter until three-quarters full. Place on plate and spoon the avocado on top so the ring is full. Smooth the surface and carefully remove the ring. Garnish with the salmon caviar.

Make some thin herb pancakes and cut into circles with a two inch ring cutter.

Place the cooked salmon on the pancake next to the avocado and crab. Drizzle a little olive oil over and garnish with the wild asparagus.

Swinfen Hall Hotel
Swinfen, nr Lichfield, Staffordshire, WS14 9RE.
Tel: 01543 481494
info@swinfenhallhotel.co.uk   www.swinfenhallhotel.co.uk

SWINFEN HALL HOTEL

Duo of Cornish lamb with tomato sorbet

INGREDIENTS

2 x 7-bone racks of lamb

Pig's caul

300ml lamb stock

100ml Madeira

Salt and pepper

Tomato sorbet

8 ripe plum tomatoes

3tbsps of glucose syrup

150ml water

Salt and pepper

Tabasco sauce

Chicken mousse

7oz chicken breast (minced)

5 cloves of lightly roasted garlic

Sprig of fresh thyme

1 egg

150ml double cream

Salt and pepper

Parmesan tuille

METHOD

For the mousse, place all the ingredients except the cream, into a food processor and blend into a smooth paste, then add the cream and blend until thickened.

Trim the meat, removing all fat and sinew, and scrape all bones. Remove four cutlets from each rack and remove the loin from each remaining piece.

Cut the cutlets into four two-bone portions and cut each loin in half.

Spoon the mousse on to one side of each cutlet and cover with a piece of the caul joining the ends at the back of the meat for presentation.

Poach the four loins in the Madeira and lamb stock for about seven minutes. Meanwhile roast the cutlets in a hot oven for 8-10 minutes, until the mousse is firm to the touch. Remove the loins from the stock and leave to rest, meanwhile reduce the stock and Madeira to make the sauce.

To make the sorbet: Put the whole tomatoes in a food processor and blend in to a pulp. Pass this through a sieve to remove the skin and seeds. Boil the water and glucose together and simmer for three minutes, then add this to the tomato pulp with a dash of Tabasco sauce; season and churn in an ice cream maker or place in the freezer and mix every 20 minutes until solid.

To serve: Place the tomato sorbet in a filo basket with a savoury Parmesan tuille.

Place the cutlets on creamed salsify and carve the loin onto mashed potato and creamed spinach.

Swinfen Hall Hotel
Swinfen, nr Lichfield, Staffordshire, WS14 9RE.
Tel: 01543 481494
info@swinfenhallhotel.co.uk   www.swinfenhallhotel.co.uk

SWINFEN HALL HOTEL

Crêpe soufflé of raspberries

4 large eggs (separated)

50g caster sugar

250g raspberries

1 pint double cream (whipped)

$1/_2$ pint raspberry coulis

Beat the yolks and half the sugar until they are pale in colour and the volume has doubled. Set aside in a bowl. Whip the egg whites with the remaining sugar until stiff. Gently fold the two mixtures together.

Spread the mixture onto a pre-heated and oiled baking tray, to a thickness of three quarters of an inch and bake until golden brown in a medium oven. When cool, cut into circles, four inches in diameter.

To assemble, pipe the whipped cream onto one of the crêpes and pile the raspberries on top. Repeat and top with another crêpe. Dust with icing sugar and pour the raspberry coulis around the base.

Garnish with a sprig of mint and serve ideally with home-made vanilla ice-cream.

Swinfen Hall Hotel
Swinfen, nr Lichfield, Staffordshire, WS14 9RE.
Tel: 01543 481494
info@swinfenhallhotel.co.uk   www.swinfenhallhotel.co.uk

THE BULL'S HEAD

THE BULL'S HEAD

The Bull's Head country pub and restaurant has been a favourite haunt of many for years.

Known far and wide for its idyllic location opposite Warwickshire's oldest Saxon Church in Wootton Wawen, its 14th century origins create an inviting atmosphere enjoyed all the more since a recent renovation and refurbishment.

The newly-designed restaurant resembles a Saxon great hall and has proved hugely popular.

We serve the very best modern British cuisine with gastronomic delights from around the world; all of this with seasonally changing menus utilising the highest quality produce to create both innovative and exciting dishes.

Our team of dedicated professionals enjoy a passion for designing mouth-watering meals, which include a variety of daily specials from exotic fish to homemade tempting desserts. Their aim is to ensure you enjoy a memorable dining experience.

Special occasions, celebrations, ladies' lunches and business lunches are all catered for with style and flair.

You can enjoy a special ambience at The Bull's Head.

Tony Murphy, proprietor

Rabbit, prune and walnut terrine

INGREDIENTS

1 rabbit, skinned and jointed (ask your butcher to do this)

12-15 rashers streaky bacon

1tsp chopped fresh thyme

150ml Armagnac or brandy

Handful of shelled walnuts

125g pitted prunes

Salt and pepper to season

Forcemeat

1 egg

125g sausage meat

Zest of 1 lemon

1tsp chopped fresh sage

Rabbit liver (chicken if preferred)

METHOD

Remove the rabbit meat from the bone and cut into strips. Season with salt and pepper. Place rabbit into a bowl with prunes, Armagnac and walnuts. Leave to marinate for two hours.

Mix together all the forcemeat ingredients and keep to one side.

Line a terrine mould with rashers which should run across the bottom and over the sides.

Start building the terrine layer by layer, alternating the two mixes.

Fold bacon rashers over to seal the terrine.

Cut a piece of cardboard to fit the top of the terrine, cover it with foil and put this on top followed by the lid.

Place the terrine into a roasting tray and make a bain marie.

Cook at 180°C or gas mark 4 for one and a quarter hours.

Allow the terrine to cool and place a weight on top to press overnight.

To serve: Slice and serve with relishes and country breads.

The Bull's Head
Stratford Road, Wootton Wawen, Solihull, B95 6BD
Tel: 01564 792511

THE BULL'S HEAD

Chicken with chorizo and herb stuffing

INGREDIENTS

4 x 8 oz chicken breast (skin on)	1tsp fresh chopped sage
160g butter	1tsp fresh chopped basil
150g diced Spanish onion	1tsp fresh chopped flat leaf parsley
100g chorizo sausage	100g breadcrumbs

METHOD

Heat the butter in a saucepan, add the onion and sweat down without browning. Add the chorizo and herbs and simmer for five minutes.

Next add the breadcrumbs and mix together well (should be a firm dough-like consistency when held). Leave to cool.

Place the chicken skin-side down on a chopping board. Insert knife into side and make a small pocket. Fill with stuffing.

Heat a medium-sized frying pan with a drizzle of olive oil and place a seasoned chicken breast in skin-side down. Cook for approx two minutes, turn over and repeat.

Place in a hot oven for approx 12-15 minutes.

To serve: with mash and a choice of vegetables.

The Bull's Head
Stratford Road, Wootton Wawen, Solihull, B95 6BD
Tel: 01564 792511

THE BULL'S HEAD

Chocolate pecan pie

INGREDIENTS

Sweet pastry

175g plain flour

100g butter

2 egg yolks

10 floz cold water

35g caster sugar

Pie filling

3 eggs (lightly beaten)

$1/3$ cup caster sugar

1 cup glucose

125g dark chocolate

30g butter

200g pecans

METHOD

First make the sweet pastry by putting all the ingredients in a bowl and forming a dough. Rest for 30 minutes, roll out and line a tart case. Blind bake for 20 minutes and set aside.

Pie mix: melt chocolate and butter together, being careful not to overheat. Set aside. Put the eggs in a bowl and whisk in the sugar. Add glucose (if too thick heat gently until pliable). Place the pecan nuts into the tart base and fill with the pie mix.

Cook in a preheated oven at 180°C or gas mark 4 for 20-30 minutes (checking the centre, which should spring to the touch, before removing).

Serve: with marscapone or freshly whipped cream.

The Bull's Head
Stratford Road, Wootton Wawen, Solihull, B95 6BD
Tel: 01564 792511

THE DURHAM OX

THE DURHAM OX

Having a well-travelled chef on board is always a bonus if you are seeking to inject some excitement into your menu.

Michael Lennon has been personal chef to King Hussein of Jordan, and worked in Mauritius, Australia and Germany, among others. He's cooked Oriental, Indian and Arabic dishes – in fact he's probably cooked his way around the world. Now he finds himself in the Warwickshire countryside where he's cooking up delights with us at the Durham Ox.

Zara Phillips famously attended the launch a year ago, which was featured in both OK and Hello magazines.

We place a strong emphasis on relaxed, informal service, but insist on well trained, enthusiastic staff with high standards of service and a flare for customer service which is why you will find the majority of our restaurant and bar staff are of foreign nationality.

The food is in the à la carte 'gastro' style, but grounded in traditional home-cooked dishes.

Michael is planning some Oriental flavours for the new menu, having spent his first year 'sorting the kitchens out' and getting things right.

Summer is the busiest time for the pub, when the al fresco dining really takes off.

The Ox is set in three acres of land and there's seating for 200 people outside, plus a 30 foot barbeque.

But inside we've retained the locals bar, known as the Tack Bar and have a 60 cover restaurant and lounge bar. We feel we offer the best of both worlds – a pub atmosphere with great food.

Ross Sanders, owner

THE DURHAM OX

Pastinni of wild mushrooms

INGREDIENTS

Serves 2

320g pastinni pasta

200g wild mushrooms

80g butter

120g rocket leaves

Parmesan rind

20g chopped garlic

40g chopped shallots

8ml truffle oil

1ltr mushroom stock

Mushroom stock

1ltr vegetable stock

50ml white wine (dry)

50g butter

300g wild mushroom trimmings

200g parmesan shavings

200g white onion, chopped

30g garlic, chopped

METHOD

Place butter in a flat bottom saucepan along with the garlic and shallots and cook until transparent.

Heat the stock until simmering, add the mushrooms and pastinni pasta to the shallot mixture and heat for two minutes.

Slowly add the stock to the pasta, one ladle at a time, making sure the pasta is absorbing the liquid before adding more. Use the same approach as for risotto, and don't use a metal spoon.

Once all the stock has been used the pasta should be tender and the mushrooms cooked.

Remove and stand for one minute. Season, plate and garnish with dressed rocket leaves and parmesan shavings. Drizzle truffle oil over the top.

Mushroom stock: Place butter, garlic, onions and mushrooms in a pan and cook on a low heat for five minutes.

Add the parmesan and vegetable stock to the pan and simmer for ten minutes. Remove from heat and add white wine.

Cool and leave in fridge overnight, then pass through a fine sieve.

The Durham Ox
Shrewley Common, Shrewley, Warwick. CV35 7AY
Tel: 01926 842283
info@durham-ox.com   www.durham-ox.com

THE DURHAM OX

Lamb noisettes with rosemary mashed potatoes

INGREDIENTS

Large shoulder of lamb, boned and rolled

100ml vegetable stock

2 anchovy fillets

4 garlic cloves

1 sprig rosemary

10 olives

8 cherry tomatoes

600g rosemary mashed potato

10ml extra virgin olive oil

60ml white wine

Rosemary mashed potatoes

600g mashed potatoes

10g chopped rosemary

60g butter

60g double cream

$1/_2$ pinch nutmeg

Pinch salt and pepper

METHOD

Place the lamb in a shallow roasting dish, along with the rosemary, garlic, wine, vegetable stock and anchovy fillets.

Season the dish with cracked black pepper and place in a preheated oven at 120°C for four hours, ensuring the liquid doesn't evaporate.

Once cooked allow to cool, drain the liquid into a small saucepan and reduce.

Remove the string from the lamb, slice into even rings and pan-fry in the butter until golden brown.

Heat the olives and tomatoes in the cooking liquer.

Heat up the rosemary mash (made earlier).

Place the mash in the centre of the plate, placing the lamb on top.

Drizzle the juices over the lamb and finish with olive oil.

Rosemary mashed potatoes: Cook the rosemary in the butter for three minutes on a slow heat.

Add the mash and stir. Add the cream and seasoning.

The Durham Ox
Shrewley Common, Shrewley, Warwick. CV35 7AY
Tel: 01926 842283
info@durham-ox.com   www.durham-ox.com

Apple tart

INGREDIENTS

1 puff pastry disc, six inches in diameter

2 Granny Smith apples

50g demerara sugar

30g butter

1 scoop vanilla ice cream

METHOD

Peel apples, cut in half and core. Place in water to avoid discolouration.

Place the sugar in a saucepan, add the apples and cook for one minute. Add the butter, turn the heat down to low then cook on a simmering heat for four minutes until the sugar starts to caramelise.

Remove from the heat and allow to cool for a couple of minutes.

Place the puff pastry disc on top of the apples and bake in a preheated oven for 12 minutes at 180ºC until the pastry is golden brown.

Once cooked place the serving dish on top of the pan and turn out the tart while still hot.

Dust with cinnamon and serve with a scoop of ice cream.

The Durham Ox
Shrewley Common, Shrewley, Warwick. CV35 7AY
Tel: 01926 842283
info@durham-ox.com   www.durham-ox.com

THE MOAT HOUSE
ACTON TRUSSEL

THE MOAT HOUSE

The Moat House has been in existence as a property since the 1500s. It's a beautiful moated manor in a beautiful setting by the Staffordshire and Worcestershire canal.

The present chapter in a long history started when the family occupied it as a farm in 1955.

During the agricultural doldrums of the 80s the family decided to diversify and developed the Moat House into a pub. Before then, Acton Trussel had been the only village for miles without one.

I came on board as manager and partner in the late 90s and together we moved the house into another sphere, expanding it into the four star private hotel it has become today. And as the hotel has expanded, the restaurant has gone from strength to strength.

It was, after all, the restaurant that established its reputation long before more recent developments. We have been awarded two AA rosettes over five years, which is a measure of the consistency of quality here.

Guests can choose between the lounge bar or the conservatory, and are comforted to know we don't use any genetically modified ingredients in our dishes. All our ingredients, where possible, are sourced locally. This has been recognised through the achievement of Best Use Of Local Food award, accredited by The NFU and the AA.

I worked with our chef Matthew Davies at the Plough and Harrow in Edgbaston, prior to that he worked at Claridges.

We can now confidently say that the restaurant is a driving force behind the whole Moat House experience.

Mark Lewis, Manager, www.moathouse.co.uk

THE MOAT HOUSE

Sole fillets with vanilla nage and seared scallops

INGREDIENTS

3 whole lemon sole, filleted, skinned and halved

12 fresh scallops

20ml vanilla nage (make in advance)

1 carrot cut into fine strips

Half a cucumber, cut into 12 pieces, each turned individually

Chervil

12 small, cooked, turned new potatoes

100g unsalted butter

50ml olive oil

500g picked, washed spinach

Vanilla nage

1 small onion chopped

1 leek chopped

1 celery stick, finely chopped

3 carrots chopped

4 cloves garlic, skinned

3 lemon slices

8 white peppercorns

$1/_2$ vanilla pod, split

1 star anise

$2^1/_2$ pints cold water

180ml white wine

Sprig parsley, tarragon, chervil

METHOD

First make the vanilla nage. Place all the chopped vegetables in a pan, add water and bring to the boil. Add all herbs, spices and vanilla and simmer for two minutes. Take from the heat, add the wine and infuse for at least four hours.

Sear the sole fillets in a hot pan and season. Remove. Sear the scallops for 30 seconds each side and season. Remove.

Thicken the nage with a little unsalted butter to emulsify.

Wilt the spinach and season. Arrange the spinach in the middle of four plates.

Warm through the potatoes and cucumber.

Divide the sole, potatoes, cucumber and scallops between each plate, dress with sauce and carrot strips as shown in photograph.

The Moat House
Lower Penkridge Road, Acton Trussel, Staffs. ST17 0RG
Tel: 01785 712217
mark@moathouse.co.uk   www.moathouse.co.uk

THE MOAT HOUSE

Confit of pork with pork fillet, creamed cabbage, apple purée and thyme jus, black pudding fritter

INGREDIENTS

16oz pork belly

250g shredded green cabbage

1$\frac{1}{2}$lb (750g) pork fillet trimmed

300g apple purée (see recipe below)

20g caster sugar

300ml veal stock

500ml white wine

10 sage leaves

4 shallots, minced

3 strands of thyme

150ml double cream

200g unsalted butter

4 x 10g black pudding pieces

200ml batter

Confit mixture

1 litre goose fat

5 garlic cloves

2 bay leaves

Veal stock

8 slices streaky bacon

METHOD

First make the confit. Melt the fat, add the stock, herbs and spices in a hot oven.

Place the tied pork belly into the fat (ask your butcher to tie it for you). Cover with tin foil. Reheat the oven to 140°C. Cook in oven, slow, for at least four hours or until tender.

Apple purée: Cut four apples (Granny Smith) in half and core. Sprinkle over a little sugar. Place on baking tray and bake until soft at 180°C. Scoop out flesh, pass through a sieve and season slightly (may need more sugar).

Pork fillet: Cut each pork fillet into four and wrap each piece of meat with two slices of bacon, season slightly. Tie in clingfilm and put in fridge for at least two hours.

Blanch the cabbage then cook in a little butter, drain, add cream, reduce and season.

Make the jus: Sweat the minced shallots in a little butter with a strand of thyme. Deglaze with white wine and reduce until four fifths. Add veal stock and reduce by at least one third, then pass through a fine sieve. Put back onto the heat, add a knob of butter and check seasoning.

Take the pork belly and slice into four equal slices. Pan fry in a little olive oil and add some veal stock. Place in oven at 190°c and cook until glazed.

Seal the pork fillet in a pan, season, cook in oven for 12-15 minutes or until cooked. Warm through the apple purée.

Place the warm cabbage mixture in the middle of four warmed plates. Place the glazed pork belly on top, then the purée, then the pork fillet.

Dip the black pudding in the batter and deep fry for two minutes.

Arrange as in photograph.

The Moat House
Lower Penkridge Road, Acton Trussel, Staffs. ST17 0RG
Tel: 01785 712217
mark@moathouse.co.uk   www.moathouse.co.uk

Warm chocolate fudge brownie with white chocolate sorbet, espresso sauce

INGREDIENTS

$3^1/_2$oz butter

6oz caster sugar

$2^1/_2$oz muscovado sugar

$4^1/_2$oz dark chocolate

1tbsp golden syrup

2 eggs

$3^1/_2$oz plain flour

2tbsp cocoa powder

$^1/_2$tsp baking powder

White chocolate sorbet

100ml water

250g caster sugar

250g white chocolate

Espresso sauce

6 egg yolks

$4^1/_2$oz caster sugar

17 fl oz milk

1 small cup espresso coffee

METHOD

Lightly grease an eight inch cake tin. Put butter, sugar, dark chocolate and syrup in a heavy based saucepan. Heat gently and mix until blended. Remove from heat.

Beat eggs, whisk in the chocolate mixture. Sieve flour, cocoa and baking powder and fold into egg and chocolate mixture.

Pour into cake tin and bake at 180ºC for 25 minutes until top is slightly crispy. Chill before cutting.

White chocolate sorbet: Boil the water and caster sugar together, add broken white chocolate, stir until melted and churn in ice cream maker until set.

Espresso sauce: Make crème anglaise by whisking sugar and eggs together. Bring the milk to the boil then slowly pour onto the egg and sugar, mixing thoroughly. Put back on to heat and cook out until sauce thickens. Pour the coffee in and mix. Chill.

To serve: Warm through the brownie, stencil plate with the sauce, place brownie on top. Quenelle the sorbet on top and present as shown.

The Moat House
Lower Penkridge Road, Acton Trussel, Staffs. ST17 0RG
Tel: 01785 712217
mark@moathouse.co.uk   www.moathouse.co.uk

THE MOAT MANOR

THE MOAT MANOR

It was during a previous life that I stumbled upon this gem lying almost dormant in the midst of 23 acres of beautiful woodland. It took nearly two years to agree terms to acquire the business.

We immediately set about restoring the premises whilst introducing an eclectic mixture of styles to cater for everyone's taste. The cocktail bar has a warm Mediterranean feel with stunning Moroccan sofas. The restaurant exudes warmth from its deep primrose and pepper red walls and a superbly elegant fireplace. The separate private dining room has the pomp and circumstance to grace any special occasion.

Today, our team of highly experienced chefs, led by Ian Buckle, prepares modern British cuisine which complements the environment we have created. We aim to excel at what we do – traditional fayre served in high quality surroundings.

The Moat Manor is a family business; a place where our team is our family and our customers become our partners and friends. As one of our friends recently said: "The meal was one of the best we have enjoyed and certainly the best we have eaten locally for many a year. The service was second to none and the ambience, décor and grounds were unbelievable".

And now, through our sister company, Chumley's, we are able to bring The Moat Manor into your home or workplace.

Nick Wormald, www.moatmanor.co.uk

A pavé of seared turbot with lemon scented samphire pan-fried scallops and basil sauce

INGREDIENTS

Sea trout, when in season, makes a perfect alternative to the turbot for this dish.

4 pieces of turbot at 120g each	1 clove of garlic
250g samphire	250ml dry white wine
12 large king scallops	50ml white wine vinegar
2 large lemons	250ml double cream
Olive oil	10 basil leaves – shredded
Salt and pepper	
2 banana shallots	

METHOD

Cut the turbot into 10cm square pieces.

Remove the roe and sinew from the scallops and season well.

Reduce 250ml white wine and 50ml white wine vinegar with the chopped banana shallot, garlic and the fish trimmings to one-third of the original amount. Add the double cream and reduce by one-half. Strain and leave to one side. Add the basil prior to serving.

Seal the seasoned turbot; cook on one side only for four to five minutes (if using sea trout, seal the fish skin side down until the skin crisps).

Turn the fish over and add the scallops. Cook the scallops for one minute on each side. Remove from the pan and allow to rest.

Add the samphire to the fish pan with 100g butter and the lemon zest. Cook until soft. Serve.

The Moat Manor
Four Ashes Road, Dorridge, Solihull. B93 8QE
Tel: 01564 779988
info@moatmanor.co.uk   www.moatmanor.co.uk

Chumley's
The Georgian House, Eagle Court, Saltisford, Warwick. CV34 4TD
Tel: 0121 353 2323
info@chumleys.uk.com   www.chumleys.uk.com

THE MOAT MANOR

A saddle of English lamb filled with wild mushrooms accompanied by dauphinoise potatoes and red wine sauce

INGREDIENTS

1 boneless saddle of lamb

500g wild mushrooms

50g chopped rosemary

50g chopped thyme

100g chopped shallots

8 large white potatoes

2 cloves of garlic – chopped

500ml double cream

150ml red wine

500ml good brown chicken stock

Salt and pepper

METHOD

Sauté all the wild mushrooms with the rosemary and thyme. Add a little of the garlic and season. Leave to cool down.

Trim the saddle of lamb removing all excess sinew. Leave enough of the outside fat to wrap around all the meat.

Fill the gap between the two pieces of meat with the wild mushrooms.

Fold over the lamb to make one large cylinder-shaped piece of meat. Tie with string to secure the filling inside.

Brown the meat all over and cook for 20 minutes at 180ºC.

Slice the potatoes thinly and place in a 10cm-deep greaseproof-lined tray. Season with garlic, salt and pepper. Pour the cream over the top. Cook until the potatoes are soft and they have browned on the top.

Reduce the red wine in a sauce pan by two-thirds. Add the chicken stock and reduce by two-thirds again. Serve.

The Moat Manor
Four Ashes Road, Dorridge, Solihull. B93 8QE
Tel: 01564 779988
info@moatmanor.co.uk   www.moatmanor.co.uk

Chumley's
The Georgian House, Eagle Court, Saltisford, Warwick. CV34 4TD
Tel: 0121 353 2323
info@chumleys.uk.com   www.chumleys.uk.com

Lemon and rosemary tart with a raspberry sorbet

INGREDIENTS

Juice and zest of 4 lemons	6 eggs
350ml double cream	40g rosemary
165g caster sugar	Pastry case

METHOD

Make syrup from the lemon juice and sugar. Allow to cool.
Bring the cream, zest and rosemary to the boil and strain.
Lightly whisk the eggs and pour the syrup and cream in. Pour into a pastry case.
Bake at 100°C for 30-40 minutes.

The Moat Manor
Four Ashes Road, Dorridge, Solihull. B93 8QE
Tel: 01564 779988
info@moatmanor.co.uk   www.moatmanor.co.uk

Chumley's
The Georgian House, Eagle Court, Saltisford, Warwick. CV34 4TD
Tel: 0121 353 2323
info@chumleys.uk.com   www.chumleys.uk.com

THE MYTTON AND MERMAID

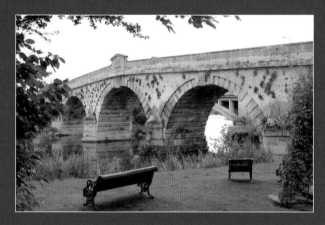

THE MYTTON AND MERMAID

The Mytton and Mermaid is a magnificent grade II listed mansion. It stands in a stunning setting on the banks of the River Severn opposite the National Trust estate of Attingham Park.

This family run hotel has recently undergone a complete renovation in an effort to recapture the charms of its original coaching inn days, reflecting an atmosphere of comfort and tranquility.

The property dates from the 1830s when it was rebuilt during the great coaching era.

It became an important posting house along the road from London to Holyhead and on to Ireland.

Originally called the Berwick Arms after Lord Berwick of Attingham Park, in the 1930s it was bought by Sir Clough Williams-Ellis, the architect famous for creating Portmeirion in North Wales.

He named it The Mytton and Mermaid. The 'Mytton' comes from John Mytton, or 'Mad' Jack Mytton, a local squire who inherited a fortune at an early age of twenty but squandered it all on wine, women and song.

The Mermaid was the crest of the Portmeirion Hotel and so The Mytton and Mermaid was born.

Our newly acquired head chef John Bradley oversees the food operation with passion and diligence, and a wealth of awards to his name including 'Cateys menu of the year', young chef of the year and recently voted the youngest masterchef in Great Britain.

With his string of rosettes and Michelin Star Accreditations, John wishes to develop and inspire the kitchen brigade into producing the finest local and freshest food.

Ann Ditella, owner, The Mytton and Mermaid

Goat's cheese fondant with cherry tomato jelly

INGREDIENTS

Fondant

500g Ragstone goat's cheese

50g butter

2 bay leaves

350ml whipping cream

3 black peppercorns

3 sprigs of thyme

Salt and pepper

Cherry tomato jelly

500g ripe vine cherry tomatoes

$1/4$ tsp saffron powder

4 tarragon leaves

3 leaves bronze gelatine

Pinch salt

METHOD

Fondant: Place all ingredients in a pan and gently simmer for 15-20 minutes.
   Remove bay leaf, thyme and peppercorns. Chill to set.

Cherry tomato jelly: Blitz all but four of the cherry tomatoes in a food processor, add the saffron and salt.
   Strain the pulp through muslin overnight in the fridge
   Soak the gelatine leaves in cold water, when soft drain and slowly bring to the boil.
   Add the gelatine to the tomato water and pour into chosen mould with one cherry tomato and a sprig of tarragon. Chill to set.

The Mytton and Mermaid
Atcham, nr Shrewsbury, Shropshire. SY5 6QG
Tel: 01743 761220
info@myttonandmermaid.co.uk   www.myttonandmermaid.co.uk

THE MYTTON AND MERMAID

Beef and kidney pie

175-200g beef fillet	Goose fat
100g kidney, cut into small dice	Shortcrust pastry
25ml Borolo wine	4 sprigs sage
50ml jus	2 shallots
75g carrot, leek, celery – small diced	1 clove garlic
Marinating oil (ground nut, extra	50g pancetta
virgin olive oil, garlic, thyme, bay leaf,	40g savoy cabbage
tsp lemon juice)	

METHOD

Wrap the fillet tightly in clingfilm to maintain its shape. Marinate in the oil for at least 48 hours. The beef should be hung for at least 14 days.

Seal the fillet in some hot goose fat, season and finish cooking in the oven at 200ºC until cooked. Turn once halfway through cooking, and continually baste in the fat.

In the same pan, fry the pancetta until golden, add the cabbage, a little water and 20ml of the jus, reduce until the cabbage is al dente.

Finely slice the shallots, fry in a little of the goose fat, add crushed garlic, add kidney, seal on all sides and add vegetables.

Deglaze with wine, add all remaining ingredients and reduce.

Serve with potato rosti and creamed celeriac.

The Mytton and Mermaid
Atcham, nr Shrewsbury, Shropshire. SY5 6QG
Tel: 01743 761220
info@myttonandmermaid.co.uk   www.myttonandmermaid.co.uk

Apple lasagne

INGREDIENTS

100g caramel

50g almonds

1kg bramley apples

METHOD

Blitz the almonds in a food processor, add the caramel and blitz to a fine dust.

Finely slice the apples with a mandolin, removing pips, and in a deep dish create an entire layer of apple slightly overlapping to cover the base of the dish.

Sprinkle with caramel dust and create a second layer of apple, continue layering until you have 12 layers, press down firmly.

Cook on 180ºC for 20 minutes, until the apple is al dente in the middle.

Remove from oven and chill.

The Mytton and Mermaid
Atcham, nr Shrewsbury, Shropshire. SY5 6QG
Tel: 01743 761220
info@myttonandmermaid.co.uk   www.myttonandmermaid.co.uk

THE OLD SCHOOL HOUSE

THE OLD SCHOOL HOUSE

We have an experienced and accomplished team working in our restaurant at The Old School House.

Exciting dishes such as fresh Scottish scallops wrapped in bacon, Barbery Duck with apricot sauce or medallion of turbot with prawns and capers are the standard diners can expect when they pay us a visit.

Constant innovations mean we are never short of inspiration where our menus are concerned. We offer a huge choice, including our renowned Caesar salad and delicious seafood dishes.

The Old School House is in the beautiful village of Weeford close to Tamworth, Lichfield and Sutton Coldfield, and as the name suggests was converted from Weeford village school.

It has been extensively refurbished, although some traces of the past remain.

One of the rooms available for wedding ceremonies is the original Headmaster's study and hence is now known as 'The Master's Room'.

The restaurant is available for conferences, business meetings and private functions, as well a superb wedding venue. And each year we host Ascot Ladies' Day in our marquee, bringing the thrill of the races a little closer to home with a gourmet three-course lunch accompanying the coverage on a large screen TV.

Dining with us, whatever the occasion, means experiencing delicious food, friendly service and excellent value for money.

Nigel Dobson, The Old School House

THE OLD SCHOOL HOUSE

School House avocado prawn salad

INGREDIENTS

Salad

1 large ripe avocado

12 pink grapefruit segments

1tbsp cottage cheese

150g prawns

Mixed salad leaves

Salad mix of sliced peppers, cucumber, and tomato

Dressing (can be made in advance)

150g fresh raspberries (frozen can be used)

3tsp raspberry vinegar (white wine vinegar can be used)

200ml olive oil

1tsp white sugar

Pinch salt

METHOD

Place a small amount of the mixed salad leaves on a plate, and place a small amount of the salad mix on top.

Place three of the grapefruit segments around the plate and between each segment place half a teaspoon of cottage cheese.

On top of the salad place a quarter of the prawns.

Cut the avocado in half and remove the stone. Peel each half, cut each half in half again and fan out and place on top of the prawns.

Using a spoon, zig zag the dressing over the top of the salad.

Dressing: Place the raspberries, vinegar, salt, and the sugar in a blender on high speed. Once well blitzed slowly add the olive oil. Strain out the pips.

Old School House
Weeford, Lichfield, Staffordshire. WS14 0PW
Tel: 01543 480009
nigel@oldschoolhouse.co.uk   www.oldschoolhouse.co.uk

THE OLD SCHOOL HOUSE

Roasted best end of lamb with parsnip mash

INGREDIENTS

4 best ends of lamb

2 cloves of garlic (roughly chopped)

450ml lamb (or beef) stock

150ml red wine

8 sprigs rosemary

1tbsp flour

$^1/_2$tbsp tomato purée

Salt and pepper

Mash

4 parsnips

1 potato

100g butter

METHOD

Peel the parsnips and the potato, roughly cut up, place into a pan of salted water and boil for about 15 minutes or until soft. Drain off the water, mash with a fork adding the butter, season to taste.

Trim the fat off the lamb and season. Place in a hot lightly oiled pan and seal the lamb then place in a roasting tray, add the garlic and half the rosemary.

Place in a hot oven (200°C gas mark 6) for about 15-20 minutes.

Take the lamb out of the oven and place on to a plate, keeping the juices in the tray.

Place the tray back onto the heat, add the red wine and bring to the boil. Boil for about 3-5 minutes.

Pour the juice and wine into a saucepan and place back on the heat, add the tomato purée and the flour and mix well. Slowly add the lamb (or beef) stock a quarter at a time bring back to the boil each time. Once all stock is added simmer for about five minutes then strain the sauce.

Place the lamb back in the oven on a low heat.

Put some of the mash on the centre of a plate.

Cut the lamb into individual cutlets and arrange around the mash. Drizzle the sauce over the lamb and garnish with a sprig of the rosemary.

Serve with vegetables of your choice.

Old School House
Weeford, Lichfield, Staffordshire. WS14 0PW
Tel: 01543 480009
nigel@oldschoolhouse.co.uk   www.oldschoolhouse.co.uk

THE OLD SCHOOL HOUSE

Mango and ginger cheesecake

INGREDIENTS

Prep Time: 10-15 minutes.
Plus 1-2 hours to set. Serves 4-8

Base
125g digestive biscuits
50g melted butter

Cheesecake mix
155g cream cheese
55g caster sugar
255g mangoes (or 1 450g tin of mangos, juice drained)
2 balls stem ginger
3 leaves of gelatine
500ml whipping cream

METHOD

Line a 2 inch individual mould with grease proof or clingfilm.

Crush the biscuits, add the melted butter and mix well.

Press in to the bottom of the mould and set aside.

Soak the gelatine in cold water.

Mix the cream cheese and the sugar until well combined.

Blitz the mangoes and the ginger, add to the cheese mix and stir in well.

Semi whip the cream until it reaches ribbon stage.

Drain off the water from the gelatine and melt (over heat or in the microwave for 30 seconds). Once melted mix well into the cream cheese mix.

Fold in the cream. Then pour on to the biscuit base. Place in the fridge for 1-2 hours to set.

The mango and ginger can be replaced by flavours of choice.

Old School House
Weeford, Lichfield, Staffordshire. WS14 0PW
Tel: 01543 480009
nigel@oldschoolhouse.co.uk   www.oldschoolhouse.co.uk

CONTRIBUTORS

Alveston Manor
Clopton Bridge, Stratford-upon-Avon,
Warwickshire. CV37 6ER
Tel: 01789 205478
gm.alvestonmanor@macdonald-hotels.co.uk
www.alvestonmanor.co.uk

Bridge 59
5 Bridgnorth Road, Compton,
Wolverhampton. WV6 8AB
Tel: 01902 759049
failonibridge59@hotmail.com

Epic' Bar Brasserie (Bromsgrove)
68 Hanbury Road, Stoke Prior, Bromsgrove,
Worcestershire. B60 4DN
Tel: 01527 871929
epic.bromsgrove@virgin.net

Kaffe Frederiques
16 High Street, Albrighton,
Wolverhampton. WV7 3JT
Tel: 01902 375522
jfrederiques@aol.co.uk

Lee Garden
50 Tamworth Street, Lichfield,
Staffs. WS13 6JP
Tel: 01543 418515

Nailcote Hall Hotel
Nailcote Lane, Berkswell, Warwickshire. CV7 7DE
Tel: 024 7646 6174
info@nailcotehall.co.uk   www.nailcotehall.co.uk

Overton Grange Hotel
Old Hereford Road, Ludlow, Shropshire. SY8 4AD
Tel: 01584 873500
info@overtongrangehotel.com

Pizza Organic
33 Jury Street, Warwick. CV34 4EH
Tel: 01926 491641
info@pizzapiazza.co.uk   www.pizza-organic.co.uk

Quarto's
Royal Shakespeare Theatre, Waterside,
Stratford-upon-Avon, Warwickshire. CV37 6BB
Tel: 01789 403415
quartos@eliance.org.uk
www.rsc.org.uk/booking/stratford/restaurantsbars/

Safe Bar & Restaurant
33 East Castle Street, Bridgnorth, Shropshire. WV16 4AM
Tel: 01746 765999

Swinfen Hall Hotel
Swinfen, nr Lichfield, Staffordshire, WS14 9RE.
Tel: 01543 481494
info@swinfenhallhotel.co.uk
www.swinfenhallhotel.co.uk

The Bull's Head
Stratford Road, Wootton Wawen, Solihull, B95 6BD
Tel: 01564 792511

The Durham Ox
Shrewley Common, Shrewley, Warwick. CV35 7AY
Tel: 01926 842283
info@durham-ox.com   www.durham-ox.com

The Moat House
Lower Penkridge Road, Acton Trussel, Staffs. ST17 0RG
Tel: 01785 712217
mark@moathouse.co.uk   www.moathouse.co.uk

The Moat Manor
Four Ashes Road, Dorridge, Solihull. B93 8QE
Tel: 01564 779988
info@moatmanor.co.uk   www.moatmanor.co.uk

The Mytton and Mermaid
Atcham, nr Shrewsbury,
Shropshire. SY5 6QG
Tel: 01743 761220
info@myttonandmermaid.co.uk
www.myttonandmermaid.co.uk

The Old School House
Weeford, Lichfield, Staffordshire. WS14 0PW
Tel: 01543 480009
nigel@oldschoolhouse.co.uk   www.oldschoolhouse.co.uk

STORE CUPBOARD

BASICS

Rice Basmati/arborio/brown
Mustard Dijon/grainy/mustard powder
Oils Olive, canola, vegetable, sesame, walnut
Vinegars Red/white wine/balsamic/Chinese rice
Flour Plain/self-raising/pasta '00'
Dried chillies
Bay leaves
Root ginger
Cous cous
Salt Sea/cooking/table
Sugar Brown/white
Tinned tomatoes
Pulses Borlotti/cannelloni/butter beans/chickpeas
Lentils Brown/red
Nuts Cashew/pistachio/walnut/almonds: blanched/whole/flaked/slivered
Coconut milk
Cooking chocolate and cocoa powder (70%)
Sauces Soya/fish/oyster
Anchovies

FRESH HERBS

Basil, coriander, rosemary, thyme, sage, bay, mint, dill

SPICES

Curry leaves, turmeric powder, cinnamon powder, clove powder, cumin seeds, nutmeg powder, chilli powder, coriander powder, coriander seeds, cardamom pods, fennel seeds, mustard seeds, caraway seeds, peppercorns, garam masala

EQUIPMENT Recommended:

Baking parchment For non-stick effect
Cake spatula For easing out cakes from tins
Casserole Preferably cast iron, 5 pint
Colander Metal, with handles
Digital scales Widely considered to be the most accurate
Draining spoon Metal, longhandled
Food processor Good quality multi-purpose
Frying pans Eight inch and ten inch
Grater Four-sided, easy to clean
Kitchen timer With alarm mechanism

Knife set Good quality: cook's knives, serrated, bread, paring, carving, palette, cleaver
Large mixing bowl Plus smaller glass bowls
Measuring jugs Two varying sizes
Pastry brush For basting
Pastry cutters Various shapes and sizes, preferably metal
Pestle and mortar Stone, not porcelain
Rolling pin Wooden
Saucepans Aluminium, stainless steel, copper-based, non-stick
Sieves Rounded/conical
Skewers metal, wooden, Tandoori Long iron rods used in the traditional clay Tandoori oven
Steamer Either freestanding or saucepan top
Sugar thermometer Essential in confectionery and some dessert making, but also useful for fat temperature
Tins, various Metal baking sheet, roasting tin, flan ring, mould, cake tins, patty tins, Springform tin, loaf tin
Whisk Balloon/electric
Wooden spoons Different sizes, plus wooden spatula

COOKING TERMS

Bain-Marie A cooking method where the dish is cooked immersed in a half-filled tin or pan of boiling water
Baste To coat during cooking
Bind To blend dry and liquid ingredients
Blanch To briefly cook in boiling water
Blister To heat the surface of an ingredient, eg peppers, until the skin blisters
Blitz To rapidly blend or heat ingredients
Brown To cook until surface starts to brown
Caramelise To heat sugar or sugar syrup until it browns to a caramel colour
Compote A thick puree of fruit
Confit A sweet 'pickle' to serve with dessert
Consomme A light clear soup/sauce
Coulis A light fruit sauce

Dice Finely chop
Flambe To flame a mixture containing alcohol
Fold To gently combine ingredients with a metal spoon or knife
Glaze To coat food with egg, milk or syrup before or after cooking
Infuse To immerse strong flavoured ingredients in hot liquid, which is then left to stand for a while eg vanilla pods in milk
Julienne Very thin slices of fruit, vegetables or herbs
Jus Clear stock or pure fruit juice
Knead A technique applied in perfecting dough, done by hand on a floured board
Macerate To steep in alcohol or syrup, in order to flavour or soften

Marinade A mixture in which meat, fish or other ingredients are soaked before cooking
Napping To coat an item with sauce
Poach To cook food at just below boiling point for a protracted time
Prove The second stage in breadmaking, where dough is allowed to rise after shaping
Reduce To boil rapidly to reduce liquid content and concentrate flavour
Saute To lightly fry
Sear To rapidly pan-cook meat at high temperature
Strain To pass liquid through a sieve to free it of lumps
Sweat To seal in a covered pan
Whipping To beat quickly with a spoon or whisk to incorporate air

GLOSSARY

Aioli Garlic mayonnaise

Almonds   Blanched – skins removed

Flaked – skins removed, flaked

Nibbled – in pieces

Ballotine Meat, fish or poultry that has been boned, stuffed, rolled and tied in a bundle

Bamboo shoots The shoots of bamboo plants, available in tins

Béchamel sauce White sauce infused with vegetables and flavourings

Bok choi Chinese cabbage, sometimes called pak choy, with a mild mustard taste

Bourguignon Foods cooked in the style of Burgandy, France

Brill supremes Brill belonging to the turbot family, supremes are the fillets

Brioche Slightly sweet French bread

Chinese party sheets Prepared pastry

Caul fat Fat lining the skin of a pig's stomach

Chervil Herb with small leaves resembling Italian flatleaf parsley

Chinese wine Available from Chinese supermarkets. Use dry sherry as substitute

Chorizo A Spanish sausage, spicy in flavour and made of ground pork

Croustillant Crisp golden pastry case

Compote A dish of fruits stewed or baked whole or in pieces with sugar

Concasse Coarsely chopped

Confit (of...) A method of cooking meat in its own fat and storing in the same

Confiture Fruit jam or preserve

Coulis General term for thick sauce or puree of fruit or vegetables

Court Bouillon Broth, or aromatic poaching liquid

Cous cous A fine cereal made from semolina

Dariole A small steep, cylindrical mould

Dauphinoise Potato dish from Dauphine in the Savoy region, sliced and cooked in cream and seasonings

Deglaze To dissolve juices in a pan with a liquid

Dulche de leche Thick caramel made from milk and sugar

Eggplant Asian term for aubergine

Estima potato A light yellow-skinned potato with firm texture and mild flavour

Foie gras Pate produced by forcefeeding ducks and geese

Forcemeat Used to stuff other foods

Five spice powder Chinese spice containing cinnamon, cloves, fennel, star anise and Sichuan peppers

Kikkoman Brand of sauce

Kumquat Tiny yellow or orange citrus fruit

Laksa Spicy fragrant soup

Langoustines Dublin bay prawns, the largest of the prawn family

Mange tout Whole pea pods, eaten young and blanched

Nage A broth

Nape To ladle sauce

Oyster sauce Rich brown sauce made from oysters, brine, soy sauce and starches

Parmesan tuille Bought or prepared basket made from parmesan and clarified butter set over a mould

Pavé Cold mousse mixture set in a square mould

Pig's Caul Lining of a pig's stomach, supplied by butchers. Soak in salt water and drain before use

Pithivier A round puff pastry tart stuffed with various fillings

Pomme fondant Creamed potato

Ricotta Mild, fresh Italian soft cheese

Root ginger Thick root of a tropical plant, can be frozen

Saffron Vibrant natural colorant, extracted from crocuses

Samphire Herb found growing on North Norfolk coast also called sea fennel

Salsify Root vegetable called the oyster plant due to slight oyster flavour

Shiitake mushrooms Pale gold in colour with a pleasantly firm texture

Skate Flat white-fleshed fish

Soy sauce Made from fermented soy beans. Use dark for extra colour, light for flavour and salty taste

Star anise Dried star-shaped fruit of the Illicium Verum tree used as a spice

Tempura Flour – light rice flour good for batters, available from Chinese supermarkets

Truffle oil Available from all good supermarkets

Vanilla pod Long brown stalk-like pod, highly fragrant

Won ton Deep fried stuffed dough parcels

Notes